BUDDHA AT THE APOCALYPSE

Wisdom Publications
199 Elm Street
Somerville MA 02144 USA
www.wisdompubs.org

Library of Congress Cataloging-in-Publication Data
Spellmeyer, Kurt.
 Buddha at the apocalypse : awakening from a culture of destruction / Kurt Spellmeyer ; foreword by Robert A.F. Thurman.
    p. cm.
 Includes bibliographical references and index.
 ISBN 0-86171-582-9 (pbk. : alk. paper)
 1. Time—Religious aspects—Buddhism. 2. Buddhism—Doctrines. 3. Time—Philosophy.
 4. Philosophy, Comparative. I. Title.
 BQ4570.T5S64 2010
 294.3'423—dc22

                             2010007094

14 13 12 11 10
5 4 3 2 1

Cover design by Phil Pascuzzo. Interior design by LC. Set in Weiss 11/15.

Wisdom Publications' books are printed on acid-free paper and meet the guidelines for permanence and durability of the Production Guidelines for Book Longevity of the Council on Library Resources.

Printed in the United States of America.

This book was produced with environmental mindfulness. We have elected to print this title on 30% PCW recycled paper. As a result, we have saved the following resources: 17 trees, 5 million BTUs of energy, 1,648 lbs. of greenhouse gases, 7,938 gallons of water, and 482 lbs. of solid waste. For more information, please visit our website, www.wisdompubs.org. This paper is also FSC certified. For more information, please visit www.fscus.org.

BUDDHA AT THE APOCALYPSE

AWAKENING FROM A CULTURE OF DESTRUCTION

KURT SPELLMEYER

FOREWORD BY ROBERT A.F. THURMAN

WISDOM PUBLICATIONS · BOSTON

A single meditation cushion, and one is completely protected,
Earth may crumble, heaven collapse—but here one is at peace.

—Xinggang,
in *Daughters of Emptiness:*
Poems of Chinese Buddhist Nuns

TABLE OF CONTENTS

FOREWORD

In a critical scene in James Cameron's blockbuster movie *Avatar*, a human character warns the aliens of the planet Pandora of the danger his people represent to all Pandoran life. "There's no green there," he says of his own home world. "They've killed their planet, their mother." And, he says, they'll do that to Pandora as well. It's a powerful artistic evocation of a future we recklessly race to bring about.

But why is this so? Why do both the masses and our dominant elite insist on self-destruction in the name of "progress"? Why do we rush lemming-like toward the precipice of ecocide, genocide, and suicide?

In this truly apocalyptic era, Kurt Spellmeyer has combined his broad and deep understanding of Western religious and philosophical literatures with his Zen learning and meditational practice to illuminate part of the answer of how we got here. He has produced an insightful analysis of what he identifies as an "apocalyptic orientation" toward time itself that has built a "mental architecture that continues to shape modern life."

Buddha at the Apocalypse is easy going, well written, and solidly reasoned—and lively in the way it interweaves Biblical analysis, Zen literature, and Western philosophy and sociology with popular culture and deep wisdom. I am delighted to greet this important and meaningful work and wish its author and many readers a fruitful walk in its garden of perceptive insights and heartfelt advice.

Robert A.F. Thurman

PREFACE

Only now, after several hundred years, is the destructiveness of our way of life starting to become apparent. Global climate change, environmental degradation, economic instability—these are just the top items on the list. But perhaps the most striking thing about it all is that our awareness of this truth has been so long in coming. Why were so few people listening? And why are so few responding even now?

One of the reasons would have to be culture. Our cultural heritage has taught us to believe that the "Forward March of Progress" is unstoppable and unequivocally good—if we just keep going straight ahead, a better life is guaranteed. A common enough sentiment, but this idea rests on another one whose significance is often overlooked.

All societies have their founding myths, and in the West ours has been the myth of what I call "Apocalyptic history." We've been taught to see our existence as a road, a journey through the ages that will lead to the transcendence of time itself. This view has its roots in many places, among them the Bible, which promises that someday "time shall be no more." The journey begins with the Creation and it ends with the Apocalypse.

Like all great myths, this one has enjoyed two lives. First, it once served as a literal truth—an account of reality. And second, it has helped to build a mental architecture that continues to shape modern life unconsciously. Even those of us who no longer believe in Adam and Eve or the return of Jesus might still assume implicitly that time is like a road moving forward to a day when everything will at last be revealed. Many secular progressives, entrepreneurs, and even scientists appear to think this way. But "progress" as such, and especially as an unequivocal good, is really an article of faith, and not at all an empirical fact.

That faith still has its fundamentalists too. As we can see from the truly massive resurgence of Apocalyptic thinking in our time, what some of us regard simply as a myth is far from dead as a literal truth. For people living in an era so complex that it threatens to tip into utter incoherence, the old notion of an underlying plan has an existential power we can't dismiss as the craziness of a few radicals. No, belief in the End Times is truly alive and well in our culture. And yet the paradigm of time as a road might prove fatal in a universe governed by complexity rather than by Providence.

In this book I argue that the culture of the West begins with a refusal of complexity, or at least a deep ambivalence about it. This refusal has made the universe a battlefield, not just between good and evil but between the apparent chaos of life on earth and God's order up in heaven. Whether we are comfortable admitting it or not, the God of the Bible sometimes uses violence to maintain a master plan in the midst of a chaotic universe.

The history of religion in the West is quite complex in its own right. As someone who was raised in the Christian faith, I still owe more than I can ever repay to the ethics of love and forgiveness that I learned from the scriptures and from the communities where my family was made welcome. And yet, as a society we'll never understand how things have gone so remarkably wrong unless we have the courage to address what is dark and dangerous in our tradition. And that understanding can be greatly helped by finding another vantage point—a new place to look back at ourselves. Buddhism, in my view, is just such a place. Buddhism might flourish in the West, or it might disappear as quickly as it came, but while it's here it can offer us another way to think about our lives in time.

This book is part of a larger multi-volume project to which a number of friends and colleagues have contributed very generously. That, of course, doesn't mean they always agreed with me. Foremost among those would be Jacky Sach, whose confidence in the basic argument encouraged me at many stages. Others who took the time to read and discuss portions of the project were Kritee, Imtiaz Rangwalla, John McClure, Richard Miller,

Dawn Skorczewski, and Raymond Baldino. I learned a great deal from every one of them. I would also like to thank Josh Bartok, my editor at Wisdom, for his advice, good humor, and, yes, real wisdom. Many thanks to you all.

INTRODUCTION:
WELCOME TO THE APOCALYPSE

With the election of Barack Obama in 2008, the United States seemed to turn a page on a period of cynicism and decline. Sixty-three million Americans cast votes for the man who had written *The Audacity of Hope*, and many of them saw the election as a referendum on a brighter future. But America's vision of the future has always been a complicated affair—a tapestry woven from many different strands.

Just two years before *The Audacity of Hope*, the publishing industry marveled at a very different phenomenon. The *Left Behind* books by Tim LaHaye and Jerry Jenkins quickly joined the ranks of the all-time bestsellers. Told through the eyes of characters who could be your neighbors or friends—a journalist, an airline pilot, a financier, a Stanford undergrad—the series retraced the Biblical events leading up to the end of the world. As each of the volumes went to press, with sales pushing toward *eighty million*, many readers feared that Armageddon might arrive before LaHaye and Jenkins finished all twelve books.

According to a Time/CNN poll in 2002, 59% of Americans accept the literal truth of the Book of Revelation.[1] It's not surprising, then, that its teachings might shape how they behave as well as how they think. *Left Behind* author Tim LaHaye has played a key role in the religious right.[2] Through the Committee to Restore American Values, he has funneled many millions of dollars to conservative activists. His Apocalyptic "End Times" theology led him to push for war against Saddam Hussein, whom he regarded as a forerunner of the Anti-Christ.[3]

Another key purveyor of Apocalyptic thinking is John Hagee, pastor of a church in San Antonio with 19,000 members, and the founder of Christians United for Israel. CUI members are convinced that by rebuilding the Temple in Jerusalem, they can initiate a chain of events that will bring about the Second Coming of Christ.[4] End Times theology has also taken hold of the U.S. military. Indeed, the Army's current Chief of Chaplains has declared that the war in Iraq was the first of the disasters that will lead to Armageddon.[5]

Apocalyptic thinking has influenced another area of our lives as well. In a famous speech deriding efforts to curb global warming, the Evangelist Jerry Falwell had this to say: "How long will the earth remain? It will remain until the new heavens and the new earth come.... The earth will go up in dissolution from severe heat. The environmentalists will be really shook up then, because God is going to blow it all away."[6]

Ever since Falwell delivered his remarks, a growing number of evangelicals have distanced themselves from his view. But virtually all of them would agree that this earth is neither our true home nor our ultimate destination. If ideas play any role in human affairs, these ideas must exert a powerful influence. These kinds of ideas matter.

They matter because their reach extends far beyond the millions of fundamentalists who cheered and wept at Mel Gibson's *Passion of the Christ*. A growing number of secular thinkers—noted scientists and social critics—have begun to speak about an approaching cataclysm. Jared Diamond, a geographer and physiologist by training, made headlines with *Collapse: How Societies Choose to Fail or Succeed*. Among the failed societies he explores, Diamond seems especially intrigued by the Maya of Central America, and he suggests that an implosion like the one they faced might be on the way for us. Other observers, such as Michael T. Klare in *Resource Wars: The New Landscape of Global Conflict*, foresee a nightmarish struggle over access to water, land, and raw materials. Just this morning an Amazon search turned up the following books among dozens of others: *The Collapse of Globalism, The Collapse of Complex Societies, The Coming Economic Collapse, The Collapse of the Common Good, The Coming Collapse of China, The Collapse of America: A Ruined State*. In the tapestry of Western culture, the audacity of hope is often interwoven with premonitions of total catastrophe.

There are, of course, good reasons to be concerned. A slight shift in the earth's mean temperature could disrupt food production on every continent. Not long ago a Pentagon study foresaw a worst-case scenario in which the lives of 400 million people would be placed at risk by climate change.[7] Combined with a global economic collapse, instability on this scale would surely lead to wars—at a moment when thermonuclear weapons have become more widely available than ever.

Meanwhile, the natural environment is approaching some kind of tipping point. The next hundred years will probably see the greatest mass extinction since the dinosaurs. If current trends continue, the polar bear, elephant, rhinoceros, and tiger will all be gone from the wild. Children born fifty years from now may doubt that such animals ever roamed the earth. The long-term consequences of the species loss are anybody's guess.

No one can dismiss the problems we now face—too many outcomes would be truly horrible. And the popularity of Apocalyptic thinking could prove to be just as dangerous as our real-world threats. If we expect collapse, then collapse may come. If we're convinced that God has preordained the End, why try to set things right?

Rejecting the End Times–mentality would seem to mean embracing its complete opposite—the belief that a brighter day lies ahead if we only dare to hope. The audacity of hope might be a beautiful idea, yet the truth is that our hopes helped to create the problems we're trying to correct. Our grandparents had high hopes for automobiles. No one imagined that car exhaust would change the composition of the atmosphere. We bombed Hiroshima hoping for an end to a long and brutal war, perhaps an end to war altogether. No one understood what it would mean to kill eighty thousand non-combatants in a few seconds. Plastics were a modern miracle. No one knew the estrogens in plastic had the power to depress sperm counts and elevate levels of obesity and cancer.

To hope for a better world is still to believe the future holds the key to our ultimate well-being. But what if the destructiveness of our way of life, unequalled in all of human history, follows directly from our worship of the future? Some of us may dream of a utopia and some may be waiting for the trumpets of doom—but throughout this book I invite you to consider that both these illusions might do violence to the world as it is here and now.

APOCALYPTIC HISTORY

Our basic way of thinking is *historical*, but perhaps not in the way we often use that word. As Westerners we've been subtly conditioned to view history in Apocalyptic terms. In Greek, the root of word *apocalypse* means "a lifting of the veil." We've been raised to think of time itself in such a way—as a process of continuous revelation that will only end when the grand design behind all of time is fulfilled.

People in other cultures gathered information about the lives of their ancestors. They grasped the logic of cause and effect, and organized their stories with beginnings, middles, and ends. Like us, they wrote historical chronicles, yet they didn't think of time as leading to a moment of complete transcendence. To them and sometimes still to us, "history" was a synonym for "the past." But the most important form of "history" in the West is all about the future. To believe in Apocalyptic history is to see events as moving forward in a preordained way, from a distinct beginning to an all-encompassing end.

Among the ancient peoples of the West, there was one group who broke decisively with the older, backward-looking notion of history. The people in question were the Jews. Their fate put them at the center of a collision of cultures, languages, and gods. The Bible depicts them as dissenters who turned their backs on one of the first experiments in urban living, the city of ancient Ur, when they followed Abraham into the desert hoping to regain the simplicity they'd lost. The simplicity, however, eluded them. Attacked over and over, enslaved and driven into exile only to return to their homeland again, the Jews embarked on an odyssey that continues to this day. How they survived when so many others disappeared is one of the Bible's most important lessons. According to the authors of the Bible, the tribes of Israel persevered by learning to embrace change.

The Jews were perhaps the first to imagine change as leading somewhere totally new. We might say that they invented "the future," at least for the

Western world. Their stroke of genius was to convince themselves that in spite of the disasters they endured, events would eventually lead them to the better place promised by their tribal god, Yahweh. That place was not just the land of Israel, however. It was also a time to come when the Jews would be as numerous as the sands of the sea. No one can say that the ancient Jews were modern, yet they took the first step toward the modern world. Through their rituals and sacred texts, they looked backward to the days of Abraham and Moses, but through prophets like Isaiah and Daniel they looked far into the future.

Christianity began as a branch of Judaism but it profoundly reconceived the Jews' invention of future thinking. The ancient Jewish vision of history stops with the restoration of Israel under the Messiah's leadership. Then, in the prophet Isaiah's words, "The Lord will guide you always; he will satisfy your needs in a sun-scorched land and will strengthen your frame. You will be like a well-watered garden, like a spring whose waters never fail."[8] This vision of history culminates in the fulfillment of God's promise to Abraham—a time of peace on earth.

But the Christian idea of history culminates in the end of time itself. The earth as we know it will be totally destroyed. Jesus will return to judge the living and the dead, who will rise from their graves as though from a sleep. A new earth will be made where the redeemed will live in ageless bodies for eternity under the dominion of Christ the King. We might say, on the one hand, that Christianity preserved the Jewish vision of temporal life as a series of revelations that would guide God's chosen people to a better day. On the other hand, the Christians added something new: the future was leading beyond history and, with it, this flawed and fallen world.

The Christian Apocalypse is ambiguous. From one vantage point, it might be understood as a teaching of indestructible hope. Even if the worst outcome of all should take place—the total destruction of everything— the whole of creation will be made anew. Yet Christ himself is the one in Revelation who orchestrates the destruction. He destroys the world to save it from sin, sacrificing things as we know them now for the sake of what they shall someday be.

In this view, salvation and destruction are the same.

THE ENCOUNTER WITH A COMPLEX UNIVERSE

For two millennia people in the West have been able to explain all events by relying on Apocalyptic history. Everything was seen as moving toward an escape from the conditions of earthly life. Even with the rise of science, this idea only grew in power and potency. It's true that early scientists challenged all kinds of dogmas and folk beliefs, but most of them still held firmly to the view that history was following God's master plan. Indeed, they thought of science as uncovering the methods God employed to accomplish his goals.

For them, the universe was totally predictable, and each unique event was no less predetermined than the ones that the scriptures had foretold. Thanks to these assumptions, early scientists could study with precision a ball in flight and the force of water moving through a pipe. But what made the thinking of such men Apocalyptic wasn't just their faith in the total regularity of the material universe. The larger program of science was also aimed at a certain kind of Apocalypse. The goal was to transcend the physical world and lift humans to a higher spiritual plane.

Today, the universe no longer seems so precisely predictable. Instead of unfolding in one straight line, we are starting to see complex events as places where different vectors of causality intersect in ways that make it harder to predict what is going to happen next. In fact, no single outcome can ever be guaranteed.

How, for example, do we calculate the shifting of a pile of sand? To predict what the whole pile will do when its mass shifts under pressure of some kind, we can't simply calculate the motion of one grain and multiply by millions. The same dilemma arises when we try to calculate the nonlinear motion of a lightning bolt, involving as it does many different combustions going off in a series that unfolds at an irregular pace. A heap of sand, a bolt of lightning, the turbulent motion of water as it moves down the bed of a rocky stream—these are everyday examples of complex, multivariant interactions that require new analytical tools. Such new tools are necessary because probabilities have replaced certainties. The one-in-a-million chance can change everything. Far from waiting for us in a preordained form, the future has become open-ended—in a word, complex.

Over the last twenty years "complexity" has been used to define a special branch of science that deals with systems of such sophistication they defy the view of time as a simple, linear story.[9] Instead of involving a single link between one cause and one effect, such systems bring together multiple events interacting with each other to produce "emergent properties." Complex systems may do things, in other words, that no one could predict just by watching them at the start of their interaction.

For people raised with Apocalyptic history, all of this might appear troubling. Apocalyptic history teaches us that nothing can ever happen unpredictably, as a product of sheer chance. Everything is preordained, if not divinely then by nature's laws or, perhaps, by the market's hidden hand. To start with total randomness but then to end with order looks like an outrageous contradiction. When we observe the coherence we see everywhere—from the activity of a colony of ants to the operation of the human brain—it seems impossible that such fine-tuning could have come about by accident.

Anthills and human brains in particular are good illustrations of complexity. Within complex systems, individual parts—whether they are ants or neural cells—demonstrate what is known as "self-organization." There's no Central Office issuing directives. Instead, the parts coordinate themselves, interacting with a collective intelligence even when the single units aren't very smart—or even sentient. Each ant's brain, for example, contains only several hundred thousand cells compared to our 100 billion. Yet a group of ants acting together can do what creatures with far larger brains need a lot of thought to accomplish. They build nurseries for their young, storage chambers for their food, and cemeteries for their dead.

Homo sapiens have assets ants completely lack (of course)—ego consciousness and language in particular—but our own mental lives would also appear to result from self-organizing processes. In much the same way as anthills grow, neural connections get forged by repetition without our prior planning or choice. No one willingly decides to have an itch, or to find a sound annoying or experience pleasure from the smell of a rose. Even the most accomplished meditators can't stop thoughts voluntarily. Our consciousness allows us to think about thinking, but consciousness itself takes form unconsciously through a process of self-organization.

Because consciousness is a complex system, it follows that the societies we've made by using it must be complex systems too. For most of human history, our cities have arisen and evolved in much the same random way as ant colonies. And just as no single intelligence planned out London, Paris, or Los Angeles, so no single mind devised our laws, our traditions of art, our cuisines, or our religions.

And now some of us have become acutely aware of complexity itself. The importance of this development can hardly be overemphasized. Indeed, our awareness of complexity may have arrived in the nick of time because our survival could depend on it.

Our encounter with complexity could produce a less destructive form of life that is also more intelligent and happier. But when we factor in our culture's legacy of Apocalyptic thinking, the odds may be stacked against it. Because of that legacy, many of us feel absolutely overwhelmed. In the case of religious fundamentalists, this might explain the tidal wave of new interest in Revelation.

If the Book of Revelation turns out to be right—or the *Left Behind* series anyway—the Apocalypse is indeed drawing near. Following the Rapture, those still here on earth may behold a pale horse whose rider is Death, and Hell may follow after him,[10] but at least we'll finally have closure. At least we'll know how the whole story ends. After centuries of twists and turns, one event will prove for all of time who was right and who was wrong. Apocalyptic history will be vindicated.

Like any first-rate story, the Book of Revelation is a dense, complicated network of plots and counterplots, metaphors and symbols that keep teasing us to make a last judgment about what it all must mean. But last judgments are just a fantasy. We can wander around in this labyrinth of words from now until the end of time. Perhaps that's what Revelation was meant to teach, but it doesn't seem to be a lesson learned by most believing readers. They're really waiting for the end to come.

But even the most secular among us aren't immune to the powerful allure of Apocalyptic thinking. Many progressives still believe that continued economic growth is the road out of global poverty. Or they're still convinced that new technology holds the key to our welfare and happiness, once and forever after. Even as the missteps and disasters mount up, their faith in the future remains as strong as ever.

Somehow, solutions will always appear, or so the thinking goes—and history will never give us problems we can't solve.

LEARNING TO LIVE IN A COMPLEX UNIVERSE: THE ZEN OF UNCERTAINTY

Problems like the ones we face today—climate change, environmental decline, political and economic instability—aren't as vexing as they seem to be simply because they pose a mortal threat. No, the Black Death, Genghis Khan, and Hernan Cortes destroyed entire civilizations. There's nothing so new about that. What makes our problems now unique is their relation to awareness itself. All of them are, in a sense, artificial. They've all been produced by the way we think. And only a change in the way we think can prevent disaster.

If our problems start with the mind itself, then the mind could lead us back from the brink. Perhaps for this reason we shouldn't be surprised that just as people in the West have started to feel utterly overwhelmed by an endless string of complicated problems, a small but growing number of them have become intrigued by traditions like Zen. Zen might be one thing our culture urgently needs.

Zen is actually all about retraining the mind to deal with life in a complex universe. Consider the ways that the worldview of Zen differs from the one created by the tradition of Apocalyptic history:

The Worldview of Apocalyptic History	The Worldview of Zen
the future and the past	the present
single cause/single effect	complex interactions
predictability	possibility
divine predestination	open-endedness
personal independence	interdependence
destruction/creation	connection
ends justify means	means are the ends

Complexity is hard to get our minds around because we keep thinking in a linear way. We reason that either something is the case, or it simply isn't. Either something will be, or it just won't. Beginning with our present circumstances, we extrapolate by imagining them as the initial point of a single line stretching out predictably forever. But this habit of extrapolation is unreliable and flawed.

With personal matters like the state of our health, or big issues like the environment, our tendency to extrapolate sets us up for all kinds of unpleasant shocks. And when it comes to profound unhappiness, waiting for the future to make our dreams come true is one of the few sure bets. In a universe where possibility rules, no one can control how events will shake out; no one can even say with certainty where they will be six months from now. And the reason is worth attending to. It's not because the future can be seen from the spot we occupy today. It's because a single future doesn't yet exist, only many possible trajectories.

Once we begin to think this way, Zen makes a great deal of sense. Rather than evading the openness of things, Zen meditation could be understood as a way of embracing it. There's a famous story about exactly that:

> Priest Kyogen said, "Zen is like a monk hanging on the branch of a tree by his teeth while perched over a steep precipice. He cannot use his hands to grasp another branch, and there's no limb to rest his feet on. Then suddenly below him another man appears and asks with the greatest urgency, "What's the use in my continuing to live?" If the monk doesn't answer the man might kill himself—and then the monk would have broken his Great Vow to help other humans in need. But if he opens his mouth to speak, he will break another vow by taking a life—in this case, his own. Now tell me, what should he do?"[11]

Unlike the Great Story that has guided the West, the one that ends with the Apocalypse, this vignette doesn't have a clear-cut resolution. No trumpets on high, no angels, no purifying fire, and no happily (or unhappily) ever after. This story concludes, well, *inconclusively*.

After hearing such a tale we might just walk away, shaking our heads about this strange thing called Zen, which responds to our uncertainty by adding even more. But on the other hand, if we sit calmly for a while, the story might begin to resonate. The whole scenario seems ridiculous. After all, how often have we found ourselves hanging from our teeth over a chasm? And yet, we've all felt something like this helplessness. Swamped by debts but stuck in a job we dream of quitting. Made so sick by chemotherapy we wish we could die, but still desperate to hold on to the threads of precious life. Disgusted by the orgy of consumer greed, yet frightened that a smaller salary will take away our only shot at the American Dream.

It wasn't a Zen master, though it surely could have been, but F. Scott Fitzgerald who gave brilliant advice when he wrote that the test of a first-rate mind is its ability to entertain two contradictory ideas at once.[12] Fitzgerald believed the novelist could show the complexity of real life in a way unavailable to philosophers, scientists, and theologians. After all, their educations had trained them to make contradictions disappear. Showing how to live *with* contradictions—that was a far more difficult job.

The secret of Fitzgerald's writing happens to be the secret of Zen as well: when we stay with our uncertainty long enough, we stop counting on a better tomorrow. What we gain is a chance to inhabit this "now" in a profoundly different way—in a way less rigid and self-deceiving, and also more alive and compassionate.

ZEN AS AN ECOLOGY OF MIND

Zen helps us meet the moment as it is by loosening the stranglehold of our preconceptions, the habits and ideas that have kept us from dealing with things as they really are. And when we meet the moment in this way, we find it's inescapably open to chance, inescapably complex.

The open-endedness of the real world requires open-mindedness from us. The term "open-mindedness" may sound trivial, and we might assume that all it takes is a little furrowing (or unfurrowing) of our brows. But observation quickly shows that open-mindedness comes to human beings with the greatest difficulty. Apocalyptic history has such enormous power because it gives the reassurance everybody craves—even when it's based on utter self-deceit. In a world where chance plays an enormous role, we try to create a collective dream of total predictability. And it's a dream that often *seems* to work. In fact, we can often make it work far too well. Most adults have a finely honed ability to screen out anything that even hints of chance. Yet if history teaches nothing else, it teaches that the past never does repeat itself. The next calamity we have to face will always be the one we couldn't foresee because it didn't fit our expectations.

The Zen response to this dilemma is to tap into the part of our minds that exists outside the collective dream we mistake for real. The Western term for that part of the mind is "the unconscious." Regrettably, thinkers in the West have often discounted the unconscious because they perceived it as a haven for illusions, dreams, and even insanity. By contrast, consciousness is regarded as an undistorted mirror of the world.

Yet the unconscious mind is the origin of much that humans value the most. You might be able to give reasons for falling in love, but most people don't reason themselves into it. Love springs up from some deeper place. The same holds true for happiness, sympathy, excitement, amusement, and the perception of beauty. These expressions of our basic human nature often assume different forms in different cultures. But their underlying universality shows that human nature is natural at its core, and also primarily unconscious. As humans we share an unconscious legacy that goes deeper than our customs and beliefs. It was there before our civilizations. It may even have been there in the course of evolution before we were fully human. For these reasons Zen uses the nature in ourselves to break free from the illusions and fears that keep us from dealing creatively with change.

Apocalyptic history teaches us that our best response to the unknown is to count on the future to behave predictably. The smart strategy is holding tight to our beliefs while pushing anomalies away. Instead of asking how new evidence fits in, this kind of thinking tries to screen it out.

When we look for examples of such thinking we can find them everywhere: in our talk shows, our politics, and our business culture. If we want to find examples of the opposite—of thinking and living in a complex way—Zen and the traditions of East Asia have a great deal to offer. But the West on its own has managed to produce at least one great example of truly complex thinking: the discipline of ecology.

Ecologists teach us to think inclusively about the systems that emerge from complex interactions. For this reason they picture time as a tree with branching limbs of increasing variation, rather than a single "is or isn't" line. Apocalyptic history chronicles events until they come to one conclusion. But ecology shows that life never stops—it never stops changing and branching off and interweaving once again.

We could say that Zen is like ecology, but that wouldn't go quite far enough. In fact, Zen *is* an ecology, but an ecology of a special kind. To the Western version of ecology Zen adds on one additional ingredient. Zen regards the mind as part of the world, and it regards the world as part of mind. Zen is an "ecology of mind," to borrow Gregory Bateson's famous phrase.[13]

Mind is world, or world is mind—whichever we way we choose to go, the truth is the same. The point was made quite effectively by a twentieth-century Zen master named Soko Morinaga, who received his first lesson in complexity many years before he eventually became the abbot of Myo-shinji temple in Japan.

During the first phase of his monastic life, Morinaga had been a conventional *unsui*, a "cloud and water person," an apprentice monk. And like all unsui he'd been assigned the mundane, unglamorous task of cleaning up. But as chance would have it, Morinaga had to do his cleaning beneath the critical eye of the master himself, the old Zuigan.

One day Morinaga had gone out with Master Zuigan to work in the temple garden, and his first thought was to make a good impression by zealously sweeping up the fallen maples leaves. "Where should I throw this trash?" the boy asked the old man, innocently enough.

"There is no such thing as trash," his teacher bellowed.

Zuigan then told Morinaga to fetch a sack, and after sifting all the leaves free from the small stones and random twigs, he stuffed them inside and trampled them down into tinder for the temple bath later on. But then to

Morinaga's amazement, Zuigan picked up the individual pebbles and instructed the novice to add them to the ones in the trenches made to catch the rain falling off the roof. Finally the old man took whatever remained—scraps of moss, bark, and twigs—and used it to fill uneven places on the garden floor.[14]

At times, anyone who's gone through Zen training has probably found the whole experience absurd—maddening if not slightly mad as well. In a world with real problems to address, who really cares if someone overlooks a few pebbles or leaves here and there? No one will ever notice anyway, except perhaps some grouchy, antiquated monk. But then, an odd change can come over you when you're fussing with the scraps of moss or the twigs. More and more the world around you starts to seem strangely, unexpectedly intimate. It's not just that you begin to care about the work: you find yourself feeling uncannily attached, as though it were your job somehow to protect these things that only hours earlier had seemed lifeless and irrelevant.

On this occasion, Zuigan taught his unsui a lesson in much more than gardening. Like most people in the modern world, whether they live in Japan or the U.S., the young Morinaga still implicitly believed that he lived in a linear universe. The way to deal with chips and pebbles that he didn't want was to assume a future he could foresee. If it's OK now, it will be OK later on—that's the beauty of extrapolation. This is the same mode of thinking we employ when we dump our raw sewage into the sea or store our nuclear waste away in steel barrels even though plutonium is toxic for 24,000 years. The whole idea of "disposability" rests on this linear habit of mind: we assume there's no chance the details that we neglect will come back to bite us later on.

Powerful forces continue to promote the mind-set of disposability. Free market economics, technology gone wild, and religious fundamentalism—all three keep our eyes fixed hypnotically on the future as we imagine it. But this habit could prove to be our fatal flaw. Counting on the future reassures because it lets us disconnect from a world of change that will always be unpredictable. Yet disconnection makes us less safe in the long run, blinding us to dangers we most need to see—dangers that a different awareness might reveal.

One purpose of Zen is to let us reconnect with events in spite of their contingency. As generations of Buddhists have learned, Zen can help us come to terms with everything our fears tell us. Once our awareness has become large enough—large enough, for instance, to take in the moss and twigs—the feelings of connection and care can outweigh the fear that makes security more important than seeing things as they are.

To understand what Zen practice really means, we have to be willing to think differently about both this world and our place in it. And when we do, we may see that it's just possible we've gotten many, many things terribly wrong. It took centuries of confusion to produce human beings who prefer narcissism to community, shopping malls to forests, and a virtual existence to the life off the screen.

So it's going to take us a little time to understand exactly how we got where we are now.

I think the best way to start will be with our culture's fear of complexity. I'm starting there because I've become convinced that the West's relationship with complexity is a deeply troubled one, so troubled that it needs some outside help. And the "help" part will be covered in Part II, where the subject will be Zen and its strategies for life in a complex universe.

But the troubled relationship will have to come first.

PART I
WORLD DESPISING

CHAPTER 1:
IN THE BEGINNING OF HISTORY

CREATION, DESTRUCTION, AND THE BIRTH OF AN APOCALYPTIC GOD

Consider the opening of what might be the most important document in Western civilization—the Book of Genesis:

> In the beginning, God created the heaven and the earth. Now the earth was formless and empty, darkness was over the surface of the deep, and the Spirit of God was moving over the waters.
>
> And God said, "Let there be light"; and there was light. God saw that the light was good.[15]

Most people know the broad outlines of the story. But probably they never stop to reflect that the most "obvious" details shouldn't be: For example, Buddhist sutras never start with the phrase "In the beginning." Nor does the Bhagavad Gita or the Qu'ran. What makes Genesis and the Bible unique is precisely their concern with time, and time begins with God himself. In fact, time and God are so closely linked we might even say that they're one and the same.

Unlike many other holy books, the Bible presents itself as a work of history—a history that claims to map the whole of time. The linkage of God with time is so obvious that almost no one ever notices, and that's a sign of its phenomenal success as fundamental "paradigm," an idea so basic to the way we think that it gives shape to thought itself. The Bible is filled with such paradigms, and together they create a mental architecture our culture has come to use automatically to make sense of events. Consider the stories of Adam and Eve, the Apple and the Tree, the Serpent, the Temptation, and the Fall. Like our conceptual DNA, these paradigms have followed us across millennia. And even though they structure our experience, they do much of their work in a subliminal way.

If Genesis is the West's most important story, its most important paradigm is this: God, who is time, also *creates*. The authors of Genesis could have envisioned God as something other than the Creator. They might have described him as the Great Immovable, but then he would have represented timelessness instead of the unfolding of time. He could have been a sky god like the Canaanite Ba'al or a sun god like the Egyptian Ra. But neither of these gods created their own domains, whereas the God of Genesis is unique because he, like time itself, brings into being absolutely everything.

The Bible teaches us that the world arose from God's creative activity. And once he got started he then called on his own creations to assist him:

> And God created great whales, and every living creature that moveth, which the waters brought forth abundantly, after their kind, and every winged fowl after his kind: and God saw that it was good. And God blessed them, saying, Be fruitful, and multiply, and fill the waters in the seas, and let fowl multiply in the earth.[16]

The injunction, "Be fruitful, and multiply," means that the fish and birds are ordered to help in their way by reproducing sexually. But God issues this command to one being other than the fish and birds. That being is Adam, the first man, who was made in God's "own image."

What the Bible means by "image" is never explained, but one possible interpretation is that man resembles God in his ability to contribute to the master plan. After all, God gives Adam an additional command beyond the one instructing him to reproduce. He says, "replenish the earth, and subdue it: and have dominion over the fish of the sea, and over the fowl of the air, and over every living thing that moveth upon the earth."[17]

The appearance of Adam, however, is followed by a fateful complication. Genesis 2:18 begins with God's discovery of Adam's loneliness. After God makes this discovery, he summons all the animals for Adam to name. Then, abruptly, God causes him to fall asleep and removes a rib in order to create the first woman, Eve.[18]

Everyone familiar with the Bible knows that Eve's creation sets into play a ruinous sequence of events. God tells Adam and Eve that they can eat from the fruit of all the trees in the Garden of Eden except for one, the Tree of the Knowledge of Good and Evil. Although he warns that consuming this fruit will kill both of them, Eve disobeys after meeting with the serpent. The serpent tells her that God has lied, and that eating the forbidden fruit won't kill her and Adam, but instead will make the two of them like gods in their own right. So she eats, and when she beckons Adam to join her, he does. Once God discovers their disobedience, he drives Man and Woman weeping through the gates of Paradise. This, of course, is the Fall.[19]

COMPLEXITY AND A DESTRUCTIVE GOD

The Fall is another paradigmatic event, and it marks a turning point for God as well as Adam and Eve. Through their disobedience, God comes face to face with the first thing in the world about which he can*not* say, "Behold, it is good." The success of his masterpiece is suddenly in doubt.

After their expulsion from Eden, Adam and Eve have a child, their son Cain, who will later kill his younger brother Abel. Just as God has expelled Adam and Eve from Eden, so does he drive Cain away from his parents and into the "land of Nod," where Cain lives as "a fugitive and wanderer [on] the earth" as a punishment for the murder.[20] As Genesis painfully illustrates, God's Creation rapidly goes downhill. Starting with disobedience and deceit, humanity descends into murder and other heinous crimes. Adam and Eve have additional children, and Cain has children as well. As the generations unfold, the situation keeps growing worse until the day arrives when God surveys his handiwork with revulsion and regret:

> And God saw that the wickedness of man was great in the earth,
> and that every imagination of the thoughts of his heart was only
> evil continually. And it repented the Lord that he had made man
> on the earth, and it grieved him at his heart. And the Lord said,
> I will destroy man whom I have created from the face of the
> earth; both man, and beast, and the creeping thing, and the fowls
> of the air; for it repenteth me that I have made them.[21]

Here God appears for the first time in a different light—no longer an embodiment of time's creative side but a disappointed Destroyer. He declares, "I will destroy man whom I have created." Only six chapters into Genesis, God floods the world and returns it to the state in which he left it on the second day. But as we know, he doesn't destroy everything. Deciding that his some of his work can be saved, God spares Noah and his family along with mating pairs of all the animals. Then God rebuilds, preserving what is good while continuing to destroy the bad.[22]

When we read Genesis carefully, the implications may be surprising. As I've said, the most important paradigms are that God is time and that he is defined by his creative activity. But if men have been made in God's image and need to follow his example, what sort of creative activity should they emulate?

God at first creates freely and expresses satisfaction, but then the plan he sets in motion starts to unfold in an unexpected way. We might say it acquires complexity. Until the disobedience of Adam and Eve, the outcome of time and God's activity could never have been in any doubt at all. But their disobedience appears to bring real openness into the scheme of things, so that many different futures become possible. To this complexity God's response is violence.

Throughout the pages of the Bible we can see creation and destruction going hand in hand. And given the importance of the Bible to the West, it's bound to have had a powerful effect on the ways we think about almost everything, even if we've never read a word of Genesis.

The Bible teaches that violence must be used whenever events deviate from God's plan, and because they deviate so often, God is depicted in various scenes as angry, disappointed, jealous, and hungry for revenge. And yet, in his effort to set things right, he's never altogether deserted by loyal men and women. After the Great Flood God eventually finds assistants he can trust to help him with his work: Abraham and his descendents, with whom God makes a special "covenant," naming them his chosen people. Because Abraham served the Lord so faithfully, God promises to protect the Jews, rescuing them from disasters and crushing their enemies in the nick of time. But the Jews' enemies are everywhere, and as we move deeper into Genesis and then into Exodus and Deuteronomy, we see less of God the benign Creator and more of an angry, destructive deity.

One example of this change appears in Exodus. In order to liberate Moses and the Jews from their Egyptian bondage, this God kills "all the first-born [children] in the land of Egypt," and later he drowns the Egyptian cavalry in its pursuit of the Jews through the Red Sea, which Moses parts miraculously in order to escape.[23]

Beginning with St. Augustine, many theologians over the centuries have argued that God's violence here is fully justified.[24] Hadn't the Egyptians enslaved the Jews, ruining their lives and thwarting God's plan? Even so, it's far from obvious that a truly loving God would have killed the first-born of *all* Egyptians, or that God was obliged to exterminate the whole Egyptian cavalry. A God capable of parting the Red Sea could certainly have stopped the cavalry some other way.

But this is not the worldview of Exodus. Following the Jew's escape from their Egyptian bondage, Moses sings ecstatically, "[Our] Lord is a man of war."[25] Nor does the violence come to a stop with the killing of the Egyptians. In fact, it just begins with that event. As Moses boasts in his song, the other enemies of Abraham's people have good reason to be afraid—the Philistines, the Edomites, the peoples of Moab and Canaan, who were already living in the area prior to the Jews' arrival. "Terror and dread will fall upon them," Moses sings, "[Because of] the power of your arm...O Lord."[26]

COMPETING VISIONS OF TIME

Just as the Bible presents us with two competing visions of God—a creative and destructive one—it offers two competing views of time as well.
On some occasions the authors of the Bible seem to think that when events
depart from God's plan, they threaten to destabilize the whole of creation.

But elsewhere the Bible represents the disorder as illusory, not real.
Behind the apparent randomness, events are actually contributing to an
endgame God knows about all along. True, the direction of these events is
seldom clear to the cast of characters, but God's plan is always leading
mankind back to the paradise it lost. Looking far into the distance, the
prophet Isaiah foresees the coming of a messiah, who will inaugurate "new
heavens and a new earth," a phrase later to be taken up by the apostle Peter
in the New Testament.[27] In this marvelous time to come, the righteous will
"be glad and rejoice forever." To Jerusalem, which will be the capitol of a
global utopia, God will "extend peace…like a river" and glory like a "flowing stream."[28]

When the Bible hints that time might be open-ended, it always fears the
ruin of God's plan or it predicts an ultimate victory ending with stasis and
closure. But the Bible never offers the view that events could be open-ended
in a positive way. Worse yet, it makes violence indispensable to the fulfillment of God's design, as we see when prophet Isaiah warns that heaven's
wrath will fall on everyone who stands in the way:

> For behold, the Lord will come with fire,
> And with His chariots like a whirlwind,
> To render His anger with fury,
> And His rebuke with flames of fire.
> For by fire and by His sword,
> The Lord will judge all flesh;
> And [those] slain [by] the Lord shall be many.[29]

This intermingling of hopefulness and malevolence, utopia and apocalypse, has become so much a part of the Western mind that it might seem
to us completely fair. Today we might suppose it makes perfect sense that

the wicked should be punished: they *deserve* to be consumed by fire and cut down by the sword. Nor might we see a contradiction in a God who creates life on the one hand, and then—despite the first commandment, "Thou shalt not kill"—urges the righteous on to murder.

Some of the Bible's many authors clearly recognized this contradiction. Isaiah's vision of divine revenge is sharply at odds with other moments in scripture such as the story of the Prodigal Son from the Gospel of Luke.[30]

According to this story, a man has two sons, and the younger of the two asks his father to give him his inheritance early, before the old man dies. In response, the father gives each son his bequest, and while the older son stays at home and continues to work on the farm, the younger one leaves and falls into a loose life that soon exhausts all his wealth. When a famine strikes and the second son is reduced to starvation, he hires himself out as a laborer in charge of feeding pigs, earning barely enough to cover the cost of the coarsest food.

One day while the second son is feeding the pigs, it suddenly occurs to him that he eats less well than the animals he cares for. "How many hired servants of my father's have bread...to spare," he reflects, "and I perish with hunger!"[31] And with that, he sets off to his father's farm, where he'll ask to be treated no better than he deserves—not as a son but simply as a lowly servant.

After traveling a great distance, the second son at last can see the landmarks of his childhood home, but even before he has reached the main house, his old father happens to notice him, and races out to embrace and shower him with kisses. The repentant son falls to his knees and confesses, "I have sinned against heaven, and in thy sight, and am no more worthy to be called thy son."[32] But the father tells his servants to fetch his best robe. Not only do they place the finest robe on the young man, but they also put shoes on his feet and a ring on his hand. Then the father orders the slaughter of their fattest calf as the main course for a celebration dinner.

Watching these events, the older son grows deeply troubled by what he perceives to be a total lack of fairness. After all, why should the one who had squandered his wealth be treated as though he had never left? Why was the second son treated, in fact, even better than the loyal son who had sweated, sown, and reaped in the father's fields all these years? Finally the older son becomes so angry that he can't bring himself to go to the feast, and when his father comes looking for him, the older son tells him how he feels: "Lo, these many years do I serve thee, [and never] transgressed at any time thy commandment…. But as soon as this thy son was come, [who] hath devoured thy living with harlots, thou hast killed for him the fatted calf."[33] To this his father answers, "Son, thou art ever with me, and all that I have is thine. [But it is fitting] that we should make merry, and be glad: for this thy brother was dead, and is alive again; and was lost, and is found."[34]

The story of the Prodigal Son expresses a morality far surpassing the vision of Isaiah. Instead of responding to the son's misdeeds with anger and revengefulness, the father completely forgives him. Even before the son has had the chance to demonstrate his change of heart, the father was already rushing to greet him with open arms. Although the son is in fact contrite, the story plainly shows that the father's response didn't depend on the son's transformation. The father would have embraced an unrepentant son just as readily as he does the son who has changed.

In the context of the Bible as a whole, this aspect of the story is remarkable. When the Prodigal Son finds a welcoming home, so too does complexity. Unlike God himself, the father doesn't choose between opposing outcomes or try to enforce a single sequence of events. Instead, he embraces whatever occurs with compassion and deep joy. If he had been the God of Genesis, Adam and Eve could have stayed in Paradise even after their mistake. With his embrace of openness, the father embodies a mentality more appropriate to life in a complex universe.

RIGHTEOUS ANGER ONCE AGAIN

Based on stories like the Prodigal Son, Christian theologians for centuries have claimed that the New Testament makes a decisive break with the morality of the Old Testament, that is, the Jewish Bible. However, the Jewish Bible doesn't present one simple moral vision. Instead, it offers two divergent images of God, confusingly woven together: one a universal creator, the other a tribal god of war. We might say that liberal Christians and liberal Jews take their cue from the moments in scripture that seem welcoming to complexity, whereas conservatives in both faiths tend to believe in a God who expects obedience and delivers punishment.

Contradictions like the ones in the Jewish Bible appear in the New Testament as well. While it is certainly the case that the Prodigal Son departs radically from the vengefulness of Isaiah, the break is far from complete. For instance, in Matthew 26:52, Jesus warns Peter against violence. "All who draw the sword will die by the sword," he declares. Yet in Matthew 10:34, Jesus says, "Do not suppose that I have come to bring peace to the earth. I did not come to bring peace, but a sword."[35]

The gospels sometimes depict Jesus in a way reminiscent of the wrathful God of Genesis, Exodus, and Isaiah, especially when Jesus encounters injustice—the bullying of the weak by the strong or the fleecing of the poor by the rich and powerful. According to the Gospel of John, when Jesus went to the temple in Jerusalem on the advent of Passover, he was shocked to see the building filled with money changers as well as dealers in the oxen, sheep, and doves that people needed to make sacrifices, a crucial part of Jewish ritual at the time. Then, as the Gospel goes on to say, "when he had made a scourge of small cords, [Jesus] drove them all out of the temple, and the sheep, and the oxen; and poured out the changers' money, and overthrew the tables; and [Jesus] said unto them that sold doves, take these things hence; make not my Father's house [a] house of merchandise."[36]

Elsewhere, too, gospel accounts of Jesus's teaching deviate rather sharply from the embrace of complexity in the story of the Prodigal Son. In Matthew, for example, Jesus presents his well-known parable of the weeds of the field. First Jesus tells the story of two men, one of whom sows a field with "good seeds." But another man, intending to do harm, comes along later and sows the field with seeds of inedible wild plants. After telling this story Jesus then provides an interpretation for his audience:

> The one who sowed the good seed is the Son of Man [Jesus].
> The field is the world, and the good seed stands for the sons of
> the kingdom. The weeds are the sons of the evil one, and the

enemy who sows them is the devil. The harvest is the end of the
age, and the harvesters are angels. As the weeds are pulled up
and burned in the fire, so it will be at the end of the age. The Son
of Man will send out his angels, and they will weed out of his
kingdom everything that causes sin and all who do evil. They
will throw them into the fiery furnace, where there will be weeping and gnashing of teeth. Then the righteous will shine like the
sun in the kingdom of their Father. He who has ears, let him
hear.[37]

The Jesus depicted here is an Apocalyptic judge who will bring justice at
the end of history, raising up the good and casting evildoers into the flames
of hell. This account of Jesus contrasts dramatically with other passages
where he urges his followers to turn the other cheek and to love their neigh-
bor, but the image of the burning weeds has left a deep impression over the
centuries.

When we set the paradigm of the burning weeds beside the story of
Prodigal Son, we can see that the New Testament repeats the same contradiction at the heart of the Jewish Bible—between a God of love and a
God of violence, and between a tolerance for complexity and the insis-
tence on one great plan.

Many Christians view the Crucifixion as the moment in time when this
contradiction gets resolved decisively in favor of God's love. As John 3:16
declares, "For God so loved the world, that he gave his only begotten
Son."[38] Yet the sacrifice of Jesus in payment for man's sins also reinstates the
logic of divine revenge. Even though God offered up his blameless son as
atonement for the sins of others, we should keep in mind that God himself
is supposed to have the power to rewrite the rulebook for the universe.
Being God, he could simply have forgiven mankind, like the father in the
story of the Prodigal Son. But he continues to demand retribution. Indeed,
he requires a blood sacrifice.[39] Sadly, even this sacrifice fails to restore balance to the scales of heaven. That is why the Apocalypse must occur.

The Bible's ultimate inability to come to terms with a complex universe
is not just a problem for believers.

It might also be the single greatest tragedy of our species' time on this planet.

UNVEILING DESTRUCTION

For better or for worse, destruction as a part of God's activity reverberates throughout the New Testament right to its close with the Book of Revelation. In fact, Revelation might even be interpreted as Genesis in reverse— Jesus's destruction of the world first fashioned by the Creator.

Ever since the Christian Bible was compiled in the first four centuries C.E., scholars have argued about the identity of Revelation's author, who is supposed to be one "John of Patmos." Christian tradition holds that John of Patmos was also the Apostle John, author of the Gospel of John, although most experts now doubt this is the case. Whoever he was, he describes a vision supposedly shown to him by the Jesus Christ who rose to heaven after his crucifixion.

As the Protestant reformer Martin Luther observed in the sixteenth century, the feverish, visionary language of Revelation is quite unlike the style of the other books of the New Testament, which present themselves as historical accounts.[40] The story told by John of Patmos is more like a dream or hallucination—or, perhaps, a nightmare. According to Revelation, John heard a voice coming out of the sky, and when he looked up to see where the voice was coming from, he saw seven golden candlesticks:

> And in the midst of the seven candlesticks [I saw] one like unto the Son of Man, clothed with a garment down to the foot, and girt about the paps with a golden girdle. His head and his hairs were white like wool, as white as snow; and his eyes were as a flame of fire; and his feet like unto fine brass, as if they burned in a furnace; and his voice as the sound of many waters. And he had in his right hand seven stars: and out of his mouth went a sharp two-edged sword: and his countenance was as the sun shineth in his strength.[41]

When John sees the risen Christ, he falls down unconscious in shock and awe. Jesus brings John back to consciousness and instructs him to record everything he sees. John is also ordered to send an account of his vision to the persecuted Christian communities in Asia Minor.

Some time after this, John is shown a mysterious scroll and, as though in a dream, he suddenly feels an urgent need to read it. The scroll remains closed to him, however, sealed with seven of the wax seals used in ancient times to secure important documents. Seeing the scroll closed but still wanting to read it, John begins to cry in frustration. Then a lamb—who is Jesus in an altered form—appears and breaks the first seal. The book opens to reveal something like a movie. Before him John beholds the terrible events that make up the Apocalypse.

What follows after the first seal breaks is a feverish pageant of destruction. This destruction begins with the appearance of four riders on different colored horses. The fourth of these, Death, rides on "a pale horse," followed by Hell, apparently in human form. As John watches, Death and Hell destroy a quarter of the earth with the "sword, famine and plague, and by the wild beasts of the earth."[42] As other seals open, more destruction takes place: "the sun became black as sackcloth…and the moon became as blood, and the stars of heaven fell unto the earth."[43]

As we've seen, the root of the word *apocalypse* refers to an "unveiling." Fittingly, what Revelation "unveils" is the whole of sweep of historical time, which it shows to be one massive war between order and disorder, and the good and the depraved. And even though the Bible tells the story of time, it concludes with the end of temporality itself. When we look back at the Bible's whole narrative, the logic of this culmination will be clear. To say, "In the beginning" would appear to imply that some sort of ending has to follow. Starting with the first words of Genesis, every word that follows seems to anticipate the complete realization of God's grand design. As Jesus announces in Revelation, "I am the Alpha and the Omega," referring to the first and final letters of the Greek alphabet.[44]

With the arrival of the Apocalypse, the whole of history comes to a close. And this is perhaps the most important paradigm of the entire Bible—that the universe is historical and that history is Apocalyptic, beginning at a certain point and ending at a certain point as well.

There can be little doubt that the Apocalypse continues to shape the thinking of Americans, both consciously and unconsciously. On television in 2003, the evangelist Pat Robertson foresaw that events leading to the End Times would soon begin. As he told the audience of his 700 *Club* TV program:

> The year 586 B.C. was the time that Nebuchadnezzar [a non-Jew] took over Jerusalem, and that condition lasted, ladies and gentlemen, until the Six Day War that took place not too long ago. When did it happen? 1967. So it's almost 2,500 years we're looking at. [In 1967 the] Jews took over Jerusalem for the first time since Nebuchadnezzar took it. Now what is the significance of all this? [In the Bible] a generation is 40 years, and [so] a clock began to tick that said there's 40 years from 1967.[45]

According to Robertson, the countdown to the Apocalypse was ordained by God to begin forty years after 1967—that is, in 2007. Since then, of course, the world remains intact, but as each new event unfolds, evangelicals have joined Robertson in combing through the pages of Revelation to find clues and parallels.

Regrettably, evangelicals aren't the only ones who do this kind of thinking. On July 24, 2006, the subject for discussion on CNN's *Paula Zahn Now* was the resilience of Hezbollah, the Shi'a militia in Lebanon. Though less numerous and far less well-equipped than the Israelis, Hezbollah surprised everyone by fighting the Israeli army to a standstill. At the start of the discussion, Zahn recapped the clash in standard TV news language:

> As we speak, Israeli troops and Hezbollah fighters are locked in a fierce battle for southern Lebanon. Hezbollah admits, it's being pushed back. But even though Israeli troops have taken a guerrilla stronghold, they're complaining of difficult terrain and constant ambushes. Hezbollah rockets keep slamming into Israeli cities and towns, meanwhile—at least 90 hit today. The pace of rocket attacks isn't slowing down, despite 13 days of Israeli airstrikes.

After this news, the first round of discussions went along predictably, with experts offering their insights on politics and military concerns. Then, about halfway through the program, Zahn took the broadcast in a different direction:

> Now, is the crisis in the Middle East predicted by the Bible? [What] does the Book of Revelation tell us about what's happening right now in the Middle East? Are we really approaching the end of the world....
>
> Take a look at the Rapture Index on the World Wide Web. It assigns numerical values to wars, earthquakes and disasters. And tonight, it's at 156, which is in the "fasten your seat belt" category. So are we really at the end of the world?[46]

The most remarkable thing about Revelation is not that true believers like Robertson continue to take it literally, but that its influence reaches into the minds of those who imagine themselves to be more or less secular. Zahn's referencing of the Rapture Index might simply have been an effort to reach out to a wider broadcast demographic. But she also encouraged her viewers to treat John's vision as more than a symbol. Zahn herself seemed to think of the Apocalypse as an event that will take place someday. This blurring of myth and history only goes to show how potent this myth remains.

Secular historians and philosophers have typically assumed that the modern world marked a break with the superstitions of the past. Leaving behind revelation and faith, the modern world turned to reason and science. But perhaps these thinkers were profoundly mistaken. Could it be the very thing that makes us see ourselves as "modern"—our confidence in progress and a better tomorrow—has always been deeply interwoven with the legacy of Revelation? Could it be that our own creativity has been fatally flawed by destructiveness?

CHAPTER 2:
WORLD DESPISING AND THE ORIGINS
OF THE MODERN WORLD

The Bible's attitude toward complexity has had far-reaching consequences. Even today the way we think is shaped by the architecture it helped to create.

The Gospel of Luke tells the story of a man who approached Jesus to complain that his brother had refused to share their joint inheritance. Because he thought that Jesus was a rabbi of great wisdom, the man asked him to intervene. But Jesus refused and instead gave the crowd a lecture on material things:

> "Therefore I tell you, do not worry about your life, what you will eat; or about your body, what you will wear. Life is more than food, and the body more than clothes. Consider the ravens: They do not sow or reap, they have no storeroom or barn; yet God feeds them. And how much more valuable you are than birds! Who of you by worrying can add a single hour to his life? Since you cannot do this very little thing, why do you worry about the rest?
>
> "Consider how the lilies grow. They do not labor or spin. Yet I tell you, not even Solomon in all his splendor was dressed like one of these. If that is how God clothes the grass of the field, which is here today, and tomorrow is thrown into the fire, how much more will he clothe you, O you of little faith! And do not set your heart on what you will eat or drink; do not worry about it. For the pagan world runs after all such things, and your Father

knows that you need them. But seek his kingdom, and these
things will be given to you as well."[47]

This is surely one of the most beautiful and moving messages in the Bible.
Using simple examples from ordinary life, Jesus tells his followers they
should worry less and trust God more. He warns them that they can lose
perspective by caring too much about day-to-day concerns, especially
financial security.

Then he offers these instructions:

> Sell your possessions and give to the poor. Provide purses for
> yourselves that will not wear out, a treasure in heaven that will not
> be exhausted, where no thief comes near and no moth destroys.
> For where your treasure is, there your heart will be also.[48]

It would be hard to overestimate the impact of these teachings. As Christianity developed over time, the entire culture of the West took its cue from
Jesus's distinction between the heavenly and earthly treasures. And the message of the two treasures seemed completely clear: don't focus on the things
of this world. Focus on the life to come.

Four centuries later, the teaching of the two treasures inspired an influential Catholic bishop in France to write a spiritual classic called *The World
Condemned*. In it, the author, whose name was Eucherius, praised what he
called *contemptu mundi*, "contempt for the world" or more simply, "world-
despising."[49]

Although we'll never know for sure, world-despising may not have been
what Jesus taught. The passage in Luke seems to indicate that far from
"despising" a world of flowers and birds, Jesus felt a deep affection for it.
And even though he emphasized the future life, he advised his followers not
to delay in coming to the aid of the poor. Yet Jesus's teaching was understood to mean that people should look at this world with real scorn.

Eucherius certainly did. He believed that if people took the gospels to
heart, they would give up altogether on earthly life and enter holy orders.
Writing from his own experience, he advised monks and nuns to guard

themselves against seduction by "fleshly lusts." The temptations of the flesh were very powerful—not only the desire for sex but for good food, a soft bed, a clean body, comfortable clothes, and a warm winter fire. Eucherius saw all of these as weapons in a "war against the soul," and he argued that the only true security came from fleeing a world that would remain unredeemed until the end of time.

At first glance, this attitude toward earthly life might seem nearly universal. It appears to turn up in ancient Greece and in the Asian world as well—especially in some parts of the Buddhist Sangha. But as we will see in chapter 3, the differences between East and West are much greater than they seem. Christian monks like Eucherius despised the world because they were convinced that a better one was already preordained. Their perspective was Apocalyptic in a way the view of Buddhist monks was not. Indeed, to Buddhist monks, the craving for a better world was one of the illusions they had to overcome.

LUTHER TRIES TO EMBRACE THE EVERYDAY LIFE

Contemptu mundi—world-despising—was a preparation for the Apocalypse which Jesus had predicted would occur during the lifetime of his followers.[50] In the sixteenth century, however, a German monk and professor of theology had nagging doubts about this attitude, so central to medieval religious life. His name was Martin Luther. Eventually his doubts grew so intense that he came to regard the Catholic Church as a wrongheaded institution. His questioning of the Church ignited the Protestant Reformation, which spread from Germany through much of Western Europe. Even though the Catholic Church survived and went on to become the largest religious community today, Luther's actions led to the emergence of a radical new view.

Indeed, no prior Christian thinker had ever held daily life in higher esteem. After he left the Catholic Church, Luther married a former nun and raised a family that brought him enormous happiness. In writings composed around this same time he argued that God had made everything on earth with an eye to ensuring the soul's salvation.[51]

As Luther grew older, however, his new religious movement experienced a series of reversals. From the time he'd first called for reform, he had consistently rebuffed Catholic authorities when they tried to strike a compromise with him. After a reluctant Church finally took steps to silence Luther's criticisms, he fought back (much as a blogger might today!) writing tracts that grew angry and provocative. Gradually, the war of ideas escalated until religious debates became entangled with political intrigues and struggles for wealth and territory.

In this climate, Luther's thinking took on an increasingly pessimistic tone. He began to sound a lot like the Book of Revelation, comparing the Pope to the Anti-Christ, and he became obsessed with dark, invisible forces. In a commentary on Galatians, Luther noted that no less a person than the Apostle Paul had believed in sorcery and even said the people of Galatia were bewitched. Echoing Paul, Luther wrote, "We are all exposed to the influence of the devil, because he is *the prince and god of the world in which we live*" (my emphasis).[52] How different these words are from those expressed in Luther's prior writings, where he affirmed that everything on earth was designed by God to save our souls.

Over the two decades following Luther's death, sectarian tensions continued to build until they exploded in a conflagration known as the Thirty Years War. By the time the war was over, 10–25% of Germany's population may have died, possibly even more. It might have been the worst slaughter Europe was to see until the World War I, and for those alive then, the experience was probably much like Iraq today. Many people grew up, or grew old and died, with the war as a constant background. No event of this magnitude and duration could have failed to change the thinking of Protestants and Catholics alike.

We can't say the Reformation *failed*—there are eight hundred million Protestants today. But it did prove unable to overcome the world-despising legacy. Instead of giving up on earthly life as monks like Eucherius had, the Protestants remained committed to this world even after all their tribulations. But they combined this world-embracing attitude with a longing for an end to history. They saw the end of time as their only hope for liberation from what we now would recognize as a

complex universe—a universe of genuine openness. Instead of abandoning the earth for heaven's sake, they wanted to bring heaven down to
earth, transforming it entirely. And that shift of perspective helped to
usher in the world we know today.

ALWAYS PREPARING FOR THE APOCALYPSE

We can't understand modern America—and its obsession with the Apocalypse—unless we recognize the contradiction at the heart of the Protestant
worldview. On one hand, daily life was a sacred obligation; on the other,
the world was still perceived to be the devil's realm. When the first Protestants came to this continent, both the world-embracing and the world-
despising strains of Christianity traveled with them.

Among the first Protestants in America were the Puritans. At the time of
their arrival here, the Puritans expected the Apocalypse to arrive at any
moment.[53] But they contemplated that eventuality with an optimism we
might find puzzling. Regarding themselves as inheritors of the same
covenant God had made with Abraham, the Puritans believed God
expected them to create the ordered, obedient life he'd desired since the
days of Adam and Eve—a way of life "purified" of sinfulness. In the words
of the Puritan John Winthrop, who led the founding of Massachusetts Bay,
the colony was to be the New Jerusalem, "a City upon a Hill" so perfect that
"the eyes of all people would be fixed upon it."[54]

But no one expected the City to last. When a purified society appeared,
Christ would return in his glory to bring a close to history. In this spirit,
William Ames, an English Puritan, boldly announced, "the end of the world
should be awaited with all longing by all believers."[55] The ideal Puritan
should live every day with the Apocalypse in view.

Strangely, individual salvation was a secondary concern. Like many Puritans, Ames didn't believe in a heaven or a hell as we now imagine them. He
thought of heaven as God's dwelling place, and he thought of hell as the
domicile of Satan and his demons. Neither place was to be the destination
of those who had recently died. Instead, the deceased would remain asleep
for the rest of time. In keeping with a strict and careful reading of the Bible,

Puritans like Ames were convinced eternal life would begin only after the Apocalypse had arrived. Then, the faithful wouldn't rise one by one to meet Jesus. All the people who have ever lived would rise together and be judged at the general resurrection.

Yet the best way to prepare for that event was not a life like the one Eucharius chose—one that retreated from earthly concerns. The City upon a Hill was supposed to be devout, just, charitable, literate, lawful, and chaste. But most of all, it was supposed to be hardworking. By treating work as a sacred duty, the Puritans saw themselves as contributing to God's own creativity. In fact, the Puritans were convinced that a person did good works more or less by "channeling" divine creative energy. Communing with God's energy made daily work the most important thing of all, even more important than formal prayer and time spent with their families.[56]

And what about those Puritans who were disinclined to the labors of the saint? The great preacher Jonathan Edwards wrote that "Slothfulness in the service of God...is as damning as open rebellion." Without "earnest labor, there is no ascending the steep and high hill of Zion."[57] For backsliders, the prospects were bleak, to say the least. As Edwards once proclaimed, those who turn from the path of the saints "are held in the hand of God, over the pit of hell." The devil "is waiting for them, hell is gaping for them, the flames gather and flash about them [to] swallow them up."[58]

The fear of hell gave these New Englanders a powerful incentive to work very, very hard. Even now, social scientists have found that a larger-than-average number of wealthy Americans continue to believe in the reality of hell.[59] Hard work had additional benefits, however, besides saving you from the eternal flames. It led to the accumulation of wealth, and over the course of two centuries, hard work and savings made New England the birthplace of American industry.

In the process of modernization, the basic values of the New Englanders gradually became more secular. Yet the difference between them and Americans today is much less significant than we might assume. Recent polls suggest, for example, that a little more than half of all our citizens still believe that humans were created as the Bible indicates. About a third believe, just as the Puritans did, that God is angry at mankind because of its sinfulness.[60] We might like to imagine that the modern world has made a fundamental break with the past, but as we shall see, this is not the case.

FROM REDEMPTION TO REVOLUTION

The Apocalypse awaited by the Puritans has yet to arrive, but a new world of sorts did indeed appear, starting in 1775 with the American War of Independence. So impressive and far reaching was the result that the next hundred years of global history became known as the "Age of Revolution." On the heels of the revolution here in the U.S., revolutions spread across the globe. This was the fulfillment of the Protestant dream of bringing heaven down to earth, though now it took on a more secular form.

The wave of change that started in the United States wouldn't be history's only surprise. It turned out that the spokesman for the Age of Revolution wasn't born on this continent at all, but in distant Germany. But even though he came from far away, that spokesman, whose name was Georg Friedrich Hegel, might well have been the truest heir of the New England Puritans. Hegel took Christian eschatology—the theological concern with the Apocalypse—and combined it with current philosophy, political theory, and science. The result was an updating of the Bible: in Hegel's work, the return to earth of Christ gets recast as a modern utopia.[61]

The early decades of the nineteenth century, the period when Hegel did his most important work, were some of the most miserable humanity has known. In Europe the frenzied growth of industry drove millions of farmers from the countryside, subjecting them to exploitation, crime, and poverty. In Asia, Africa, and South America, conquest and colonization by the West had reduced whole continents to abject servitude. Faced with this depressing reality, Hegel set out to pioneer a new science of world events that would rise above the pain and confusion. He felt sure that history must follow natural laws no different from the laws of physics or chemistry. And in a series of highly technical works—with daunting titles like *The Phenomenology of Spirit*—Hegel claimed to have found those very laws.

Even though Hegel had turned his back on the piety of his Lutheran childhood, his new system owed almost everything to the paradigm of the

Apocalypse. He came to view all of history as a series of revelations like those in the Bible. These revelations/revolutions would keep happening until humanity was completely unified with what Hegel called "Absolute Spirit"— a modernized version of Christ's Kingdom on earth.[62] According to Hegel, at that glorious moment, all knowledge, wisdom, power, and freedom would converge. Everything would be revealed to humankind, and our hearts would be set free from the last vestiges of ignorance, fear, and selfishness.

Hegel's updating of the End Times idea was powerful stuff indeed, and it deeply influenced countless people around the world. Whether or not we have heard Hegel's name, many of us who are alive today—and certainly most Americans—believe that history is following a plan. We think of the quest for progress as a moral duty. Many of us are entirely convinced that by means of reason, hard work, and God's grace, we can create something very close to a paradise on earth.

No less prominent a person than George W. Bush sounded a distinctly Hegelian note in his 2005 State of the Union speech, when he proclaimed, "The road of Providence is uneven and unpredictable, yet we know where it leads: It leads to freedom."[63] Hegel would have nodded warmly in assent. But most of those tuned in to the President that night, and certainly the President himself, would have been shocked if they only knew how closely Mr. Bush's vision of history paralleled the thinking of Hegel's greatest disciple. That disciple was Karl Marx.

MODERN MESSIAHS

Along with the American President, Marx shared the conviction that history wasn't a mere string of accidents. No, like a prophet in the Bible Marx believed that he could see the future to the very end. The meek would inherit the earth, Jesus said. In the same spirit Marx prophesied that the working class would eventually become the masters of the industrial world.[64] And when the workers came into their own, all the old distinctions of status, wealth, and power would be gone forever. People would contribute time and energy within the limits of their abilities, and each person would receive appropriate care, according to his or her needs.

But Marx seems never to have believed this transition would happen peacefully. He observed that different classes always seem to clash over opportunities, resources, and rights. Like the vengeful Christ of Revelation, history would unleash fierce angels to cleanse the fallen world with fire. In the eighty years that followed Marx's death, his foremost disciples—Lenin, Stalin, and Mao—assumed that destruction was the price to be paid to create a better world.

Even now, historians tend to downplay the amazing success of the lineage that extends from Hegel to his student Marx and then on to Marx's various followers. But historians have also underplayed another element of this tradition—its religious underpinnings.[65]

Writing in 1937 about the origins of Russian Communism, the exiled Russian philosopher Nicolas Berdyaev described the connection quite lucidly. Why, he asked, did Communism first spring up on Russian soil? He concluded that the Russian people have always seen their country as a "messianic" nation. In their eyes they were nothing less than "the Third Rome," the last truly "Christian Kingdom." For them, Marx's teachings added little that was truly new. The gospel of Marx only seemed to modernize the old Apocalyptic mentality"[66]

At this point, however, it's important to point out that Marx and Lenin, and later Stalin, weren't Christians and that the Christian faith was not responsible for the brutalities of Russian Communism, which set out to annihilate Christianity in the Soviet Union and sent thousands of believers to their deaths. Nevertheless, the tradition of Apocalyptic thinking, which combines a vision of progressive change with a spirit of punitive violence, helped to create enduring paradigms that were drawn on again and again by leaders who saw themselves as completely rational and modern.

And Lenin was hardly the only leader of his day who viewed himself as a messiah. The same might be said of Hitler. From his upbringing in Catholic Austria, Hitler inherited the key paradigms that encouraged him to understand his turbulent era in Apocalyptic terms. So too did the German people who supported him. Whether he was actually sincere or not, Hitler managed to depict the confusion of his time as a moral crisis that required a massive spiritual revival. In his efforts to spark this revival, he combined elements of Christianity with pre-Christian paganism, German medievalism, and the pseudoscience of race. According to the historian David Redles, Hitler genuinely "believed in a coming final war between the forces of light (Aryans) and those of darkness (Jews), a war that was to be a war of extermination and that was to occur in their lifetime. Either the Jews or the world would be exterminated. Exactly how this was to take place was left, to some extent, to the force of Providence."[67]

As an underlying architecture of thought, the myth of the Apocalypse always calls for a total solution. Nothing less than a new world order will do. In Christian scripture, however, the violence of the change is counterbalanced by powerful ethical restraints. "All they that take the sword shall perish with the sword." "Judge not, and ye shall not be judged." "He that is without sin among you, let him first cast a stone." "Whoever slaps you on your right cheek, turn the other to him also." "As ye would that men should do to you, do ye also to them likewise."[68] But as the Apocalyptic vision moved off the pages of Revelation and into the world of modern politics, the ethical restraints fell away. This change set free the destructive energy of idealists across the globe, always acting in the name of a better world to come.

BRAVE NEW AMERICAN WORLD

If any year seemed likely to bring the end of time, it would have to be 1939. In mid-November of 1938, the Nazis instigated Kristallnacht, a massive pogrom that destroyed scores of synagogues and countless Jewish homes and businesses. About 30,000 Jews were detained and sent to concentration camps. A little more than four months after that, German troops marched into Czechoslovakia. In May, Hitler and Mussolini signed a mutual defense pact, and on September 1, Nazi tanks rolled into Poland.

The Old World was slipping into darkness, but life in the New World was beginning to look remarkably bright. Emerging from the Great Depression, the United States had started to believe again in the promise of the City upon a Hill. At the moment when Hitler readied German troops for the war with England and France, more than thirty million Americans were making a pilgrimage to Flushing Meadows, New York. There they had a chance to see with marveling eyes the white and glowing World of Tomorrow.

What they beheld was beautiful and astonishing: the human spirit set free in architecture, technology, and industrial design. With its gigantic white Trilon and Perisphere, its illuminated, glass-covered buildings and curving, elevated roadways, the fairgrounds looked indeed like something from another time.

One of the most popular exhibits was General Electric's Futurama, a 36,000-square-foot model representing the future United States in the year 1960, replete with clean, efficient cities ringed by spacious high-tech homes. Visitors to the Westinghouse Pavilion were greeted by Elektro, a jocular golden robot. And not far away, in the RCA building, visitors could see another amazing innovation, a device that transmitted moving images along with accompanying sound. The World of Tomorrow might well have been the Bible's New Jerusalem—brought to you by the corporations.[69]

The agendas of the Axis Powers and the World's Fair weren't at all the same. When the Nazi Party faithful went to Nuremberg, they came by the thousands in uniform, saluting their Führer with a synchronization that turned them into one great machine. By contrast, Americans visited the World's Fair as individuals, couples, or families, and mostly in civilian clothes. They bought tickets to get in, and once inside, they were free to amuse themselves any way they pleased. They could visit Democricity or get a meal. They could even gawk at topless dancing girls while enjoying a beer. The Nazis and corporate America also had different visions of the world to come—different and incompatible. "One Reich, One Folk, One Führer" was the Nazis' motto. "Peace and Prosperity" were the watchwords of the Fair.

Still, the new America was destructive in a way that the war in Europe made it hard to recognize. Yet one observer saw this destructiveness quite clearly. That was Joseph Schumpeter, a leading postwar economist. Schumpeter wasn't disapproving, however. He didn't see destruction as an evil in itself, provided it was used in the proper way—in other words, creatively. According to him, the best future for mankind lay with the capitalist system, and he saw it as a system without parallel in all of history.

Schumpeter observed that other, earlier systems had tried to keep every-thing more or less the same. To survive, these systems needed stability. But Schumpeter maintained the free market operates in the very opposite way—constantly changing everything through what he called "creative destruction."[70]

Today, of course, we inhabit Schumpeter's world. In the lifetimes of our grandparents, the general stores of small-town America gave way to an A&P, a hardware store, a clothing store, and other specialties. Now change sweeps all of these away when a Walmart lands on the edge of town, wip-ing out most of the specialty stores and leaving the A&P to fight for its life. This is the marketplace destroying—like God—even while it creates.

Of course, the market system changes more than stores. Schumpeter might have been prescient, but he overlooked a few crucial details. He never understood that destroying to create wasn't as original he assumed, but simply a new expression of an old idea—an idea reaching back to Gen-esis. Nor did he contemplate the likelihood that the endless destruction might extend beyond finance into politics, culture, international relations, and finally, the environment, where it would threaten to unweave the fab-ric of organic life itself.

Someone, though, noticed that possibility, less than a decade later.

CREATIVELY DESTROYING THE NATURAL WORLD

The year 1962 saw the publication of Rachel Carson's bestseller *Silent Spring*. Carson was one of the first scientists to raise alarms about the possibility of an environmental collapse. From her book many readers learned to see the natural world as a complex system in which every part affected all the oth-ers. As Carson showed, spraying elms to kill insect pests would prevent the robins that ate the poisoned bugs from hatching their eggs the following year. In a simple and dramatic way, Carson taught that starting with one simple act, a web of consequences could widely spread.[71]

Despite the book's almost immediate success, not everyone applauded Carson's efforts. Her criticism of synthetic pesticides made her the target of a campaign financed by Monsanto, American Cyanamid, and other cor-

porations.[72] The motives of the chemical industry are self-evident, but some
of the hostility to Carson's argument had a deeper source. Not only did
she question the use of DDT, she also raised doubts about the blind pursuit
of progress itself, which most Americans had come to see as the eleventh
commandment. Since divine providence had favored the U.S., how could
our pursuit of progress ever be bad?

The questioning didn't stop with Carson's book. In the spring of 1967,
an article appeared in *Science* magazine that sparked a debate raging on even
now. The article wasn't about DDT. It addressed the Christian religion's
role in the destruction of the environment.

The author was the historian Lynn White, and he made the shocking
accusation that Christianity was to blame for the coming ecological collapse.[73] Christianity, he wrote, is the most human-centered faith the world
has ever seen. It's also, he alleged, the religion with the least regard for the
natural world. Not only did the Bible establish a split between man and the
rest of creation, it "also insisted that it is God's will that man exploit nature
for his proper ends."

In the forty years that followed on the publication of White's article,
countless theologians and historians have leapt to Christianity's defense. It
is certainly true, they were willing to concede, that God in Genesis gives
Adam and Eve dominion over the natural world, commanding them after
they leave Eden to toil and "subdue the earth." Yet God also charged them,
at least implicitly, to be good stewards of His Creation. Defenders of the
faith have pointed out as well that Genesis is only one book in a complex and
compendious collection. With its detailed attention to plants and animals,
to the seasons and to geography, the Bible, taken as a whole, strongly suggests that its writers loved what they observed in their natural surroundings.

In all the smoke and dust raised by White's argument, both he and his
opponents overlooked what might have been a more important point. The
real problem wasn't that Christianity deserves special blame for ecological
decline, but that a growing number of Americans had begun trying to sanc-
tify life by embracing their possessions. They were—and still are—trying
to escape the legacy of world-despising, but their solution only reinstates
that paradigm in a new and seductive way. The earth seen by Adam on the

eighth day is now getting bulldozed to clear the way for an Eden of enormous homes, lawn furniture, backyard pools, and SUVs.

FROM DELIVERANCE TO DELIVERY: CHRISTIANITY BECOMES A CARGO CULT

Under the growing sway of commercial culture, and still traumatized by the Great Depression and World War II, American Christianity abandoned its long held ambivalence about material wealth and openly became an enthusiastic promoter. Today, the names of churches across America include the phrase "Abundant Life," which refers to John 10:10, where Jesus says, "I have come that they may have life, and have it abundantly."[74]

Anyone who bothers to read John 10 can see that this statement has nothing to do with the acquisition of material wealth. On the subject of wealth, however, Jesus does indeed have much to say. In Mark 10:25, for example, he declares, "It is easier for a camel to go through the eye of a needle than for a rich man to enter the Kingdom of God." In Luke 6:20, he teaches, "Blessed are you who are poor, for yours is the Kingdom of God." In Matthew 6:24, he proclaims unambiguously, "You cannot serve both God and Money."[75]

But "abundant life" of the material kind was the theme of the 1939 World's Fair. In its aftermath, many Americans have come to accept what is now called "prosperity theology," which holds that wealth follows from obedience to God. This dogma has its roots in various Protestant sects, especially the Puritans, but under the sway of the corporate state, the fine points of Protestant tradition dropped away, and what remains might in all fairness be described as a "cargo cult."

The cargo cults of Melanesia have attracted much attention over the years, especially right after World War II, when servicemen returned to the United States with stories about a strange new religion in the highland villages. For these war-weary American GI's, the religious practices of Pacific Islanders could hardly have seemed more distant from church services back in Nevada or Ohio. Conversely, the lives of the Melanesians, who still carried spears and wore feathers in their hair, could not have seemed any farther removed from the futuristic vision that rose up in Flushing Meadows. But were the two really so different?

These Melanesians had fallen prey to a bizarre illusion. If only their faith were strong enough, God would send them modern "cargo" from the far-away homeland of the white GI's—items like food, clothing, jewelry, and tools. Some evidence suggests that these so-called "cults" began in the early nineteenth century when Christian missionaries offered free gifts to win the islanders' trust, or promised the gifts in exchange for conversion. As the Melanesians became more familiar with both Western religion and man-ufactured goods, their ideas about the future started to take on an Apoca-lyptic tone. Among the many things the Second Coming would bring, manufactured items would be high on the list.

In 1984 a missionary observed this example of the cargo religion:

> Some spirits told a young man, in the village of Papasena, that Jesus was ready to come back and bring independence and free-dom to Irian Jaya along with great wealth for all the people. He was further instructed by Jesus himself that everyone, without exception, was: (1) to publicly confess all sins, (2) to do no hunt-ing in the morning hours, (3) to keep all grave sites immaculately clean, (4) to drink a specially prepared "holy water," and (5) to be baptized by a Western missionary. If all these injunctions were followed, then in just a few days, unspeakable wealth, which is now only enjoyed by their ancestors and Westerners, would pour out of the graves. A mock radio transmitter was built at the graves to receive further word from the spirits about the coming of this great wealth. The church became alive with activity as hundreds stepped forward to confess their sins and be baptized.[76]

The idea of fake transmitters wired to graves seems so weird that it tends to reinforce Western clichés about "primitives" who are less "advanced" than we are today. But imagine how this account would strike us if it were only slightly revised:

In a vision, an angel told a young man in Cincinnati, Ohio, that
Jesus would save his family from unemployment and poverty, and
restore his deteriorating neighborhood. He was further instructed
by Jesus himself that everyone in his family and all his neighbors, without exception, were do the following: (1) acknowledge
to God their sinfulness, (2) gather for scripture study and prayer
in the morning hours before leaving to look for a job or go to
school, (3) work hard, (4) avoid alcohol, gambling, and impure
thoughts, and (5) go to church each week. If all these injunctions
were followed, then the family would be rewarded with the peace
and freedom from financial insecurity which are now enjoyed
only by the rich and by the ranks of the saved in heaven. Daily
Bible study will provide further guidance about how to gain
access to this new abundant life.

These slight revisions only indicate how closely our religious life resembles the Melanesian cargo cults. Of course, people pray for wealth the
whole world over—not just Melanesians or Americans. What seems
uniquely Western, though, is the coupling of this wish for more and more
with an Apocalyptic vision of time.

Ironically, our fusion of the market and religion may lead to an Apocalypse rather different from the one the Bible foretells. In this very real Apocalypse, no heavenly horsemen will ever arrive, no angels with trumpets, no
judgment day. Just the gradual extinction of all life on earth, and its replace-
ment by an endless menagerie of aging, irrelevant objects, along with the
trash and toxins left from their creation. Herein all the prophecies end.

We need to find another way.

PART II
WORLD EMBRACING

CHAPTER 3:
AN END TO HISTORY,
AN END TO SUFFERING

DESTROYING FIRES, EAST AND WEST

Apocalyptic thinking has become so much a fixture of our minds that we might assume people everywhere hold the same beliefs. Our sense of time seems so obvious, it must be universal. And when we turn to Buddhist teachings, they appear to strengthen this assumption. Buddhism also seems to include something like the Christian Apocalypse. Indeed, the Buddhist version of the End is even more elaborate than the Christian one. It is, however, ultimately quite dissimilar.

As a *maha kalpa* or "great cycle" winds down, a series of destructions are supposed to take place in a universe that dwarfs its Christian counterpart with its vastness and complication.[77] The end of the world in Buddhism starts with many different hallmarks of decay, but finally a fire will arise to destroy everything in the lower realms, surging upward like a thermonuclear bomb until its flames stop at the very edge of a realm accessible only to those who are advanced at meditation. Then, the second cycle of destruction will bring water to dissolve all that remains up to the next level in the hierarchy. A third destruction follows after that—this time from the cosmic wind—taking the destruction up another level yet. Only the highest heavens will survive, while the physical universe will be completely gone.

About the beginning and the end of the world, the Buddha himself refused to speculate, at least judging from the Pali sutras which comprise the earliest records of his teachings.[78] In the Vinaya, however, he foresees that at the end of five hundred years, the dharma—his teaching—will vanish from the earth.[79] Taking its cue from these brief remarks, Buddhist thinkers over the centuries developed an elaborate account of how our world will someday cease to be. Eventually, the span of five centuries indicated by the Buddha was telescoped out another thousand years. The first five hundred years were now thought to be the age of the genuine Dharma. The second five hundred were the age of decline, and the last five hundred were supposed to be the age of degeneration, at the end of which the true Dharma would disappear. Of course the Buddha's teachings have survived well beyond the predicted expiration date, and so the prophecy has come to seem archaic or opaque.

Still, anxieties about the End Times play a role in the Mahayana sutras most revered by the schools of Buddhism that found a home in China, Japan, Korea, and Vietnam. In the Diamond Sutra, for example, the Buddha's disciple Subhuti asks, "In times to come, will there be beings who, when they hear these teachings, have real faith and confidence in them?"

To this the Buddha answers, "Subhuti, do not utter such words! Five hundred years after the passing of the Tathagata, there will be beings who, having practiced rules of morality and being possessed of merit, happen to hear of these statements and will understand their truth. Such beings, you should know, have planted their root of merit not only under one, two, three, four, or five Buddhas [in kalpas past], but under countless Buddhas."[80]

The Lotus Sutra also views the world-ending age with the greatest urgency, along with the salvation of the last living beings, including the deceased who will remain in one of various hells burning off their evil karma. In lines well-known to Buddhists of many different schools, the bodhisattvas take a solemn vow not to cease their efforts to save everyone even in the last and worst of the three ages:

> Please do not worry,
> After the Buddha's extinction,
> In a frightful and evil age
> We will teach everywhere.

Though many ignorant people
Will curse us and abuse us
Or attack us with swords and sticks
We will endure it all.[81]

These lines might have a familiar ring. If we substitute the phrase "Jesus's death" for "the Buddha's extinction," words like the ones in the stanzas above might look right at home in the Bible. And as Revelation prophecies, in the final days there will certainly be those who remain faithful to God's plan.

Yet the similarities may not be as great as the parallel suggests. If we turn to a story from the Zen school, we might begin to notice some differences:

A monk asked Daizui, "When the kalpa fire flares up and the great cosmos is destroyed, I wonder, will *it* perish or, or will it not?" Daizui said, "It will perish."[82]

Clearly the student is referring to the first of the destructions scheduled to arrive at the maha kalpa's close. But as is so often the case with Zen, what appears perfectly obvious at first becomes increasingly unclear. Even once we've mastered the cosmology, we may not appreciate all that's going on in this brief exchange.

In the tenth century when Daizui lived, Chinese Buddhists might have trembled with fear at the signs of a world growing worse every day, but they all understood that the end of their time wouldn't be the end of time itself. No, such a final ending could never occur. Even with the fire, water, wind, and the rest, the architecture of Buddhist thought told them that at their maha kalpa's end, a whole new cosmos would start up again. Once this new cosmos had emerged like a flower, it would unfold in a pristine state, followed by a period of decline and then a return to nothingness—over and over, forever. It wouldn't be true, as it is in Revelation, that time would finally come to a stop. In fact, time would go on interminably.

And so when Daizui is asked about the End, it's curious he doesn't exhort the monk to practice meditation until he can ascend to the heavens far above the coming conflagration. Even more curious is his claim that the fire will in fact consume everything. Surely Daizui studied Buddhist cosmology when he was a novice in the monastery. Why doesn't he just tell his student to relax, since the topmost levels will survive, and a new universe is sure to arise even when the current one is gone? And when the new universe appears, won't there be a new Buddha too, guiding people then to enlightenment?

To appreciate what Daizui doesn't say, we need to understand that Zen masters tend to think about time very much as the Buddha did himself. That is, they tend to look at cosmology—along with other products of abstract thought—in a manner that can't be properly described as either belief or disbelief. Like so many Zen stories, this one asks a question that works a bit like a trap, depending as it does on assumptions that might be completely unjustified. By trapping us, and forcing us to look again at our direct experience, the stories in Zen try to nudge us past the terms of the question itself.

The nudge in the story comes from a few odd details. What exactly does the monk mean by "it" when he asks, "will it perish or not"? Perhaps "it" refers to something like the Christian soul, living on forever even after the End. Perhaps it means something like God's plan in Genesis, which no power can prevent from unfolding as decreed. Or possibly the monk means "enlightenment," imagined as existing on another plane, eternal and unchanging. Perhaps the student doesn't really know what "it" might mean. Maybe he's just bluffing, and then Daizui calls his bluff.

Yet to think along these lines is still to get enmeshed in the question's crafty snares, when the question itself might be the wrong one to ask. By telling the monk that "it" will perish too, Daizui could be pointing to an experience of time quite different from the one monk is contemplating—and different from the one in the Bible as well.

TIME AS A GETAWAY VEHICLE

The West thinks of time as a straight line, whereas Buddhists think of it as cyclical. Christians see the universe as a one-time affair. Buddhist see many universes in succession, and many existing simultaneously. Genesis depicts this world as the sole stage on which all events of importance take place, whereas the Buddhists presuppose worlds too numerous to count—like the sands of the Ganges, as the sutras say. These comparisons are easy to set up and they help us feel our way around some very unfamiliar terrain. But they can't do what Zen typically wants us to—testing our so-called "reality."

We could spend hours contrasting the details of Revelation to its Buddhist counterparts. But instead we might put our time to better use by asking ourselves why it is that people everywhere—East and West, North and South—appear to be obsessed with the world's annihilation.

Here's one possibility. When we read the Book of Revelation or we contemplate the spectacle of kalpa fires, are we *really* terrified? Or are we just pretending to be afraid, like watching a scary movie? Maybe the destruction lets us off the hook. Perhaps the wrathful God of Genesis is actually releasing us from a kind of jail. As the nightmarish images pile up, maybe the destruction doesn't make us recoil. Maybe we find it fascinating because it promises us in an implicit way that there's an escape from all of this—the money problems and the stress at work, the kids getting bad grades in their senior year, the medical bills we don't know how to pay. Who wouldn't want this crazy world to end—for a while anyway, and especially if we can get a better deal after all the destruction is done?

When I was a choir boy fifty years ago, we used to sing a hymn composed in 1929 by a Southern Baptist, Albert E. Brumley. Part of the hymn goes like this:

> Some glad morning when this life is o'er, I'll fly away;
> To a home on God's celestial shore, I'll fly away.
> I'll fly away, Oh Glory
> I'll fly away; (in the morning)
> When I die, Hallelujah, by and by.
> I'll fly away (I'll fly away).
> When the shadows of this life have gone, I'll fly away;
> Like a bird from prison bars has flown, I'll fly away.[83]

The hymn is less than a century old, but it's often mistaken for a classic. There's something universal about the refrain: "I'll fly away…. I'll fly away." In fact, it's the most recorded gospel song ever. Flying away is a beautiful idea. As I learned in Sunday school, Brumley's parents worked as tenant farmers in Depression-era Oklahoma. They had him chopping cotton when he was just a boy. It makes sense that Brumley might have seen his time on earth as something like a term in jail, and that he would have dreamed of a better world when he felt tired or let down.

But the Buddhist paradigm of the world-ending age shows that Asians more than a thousand years ago, like a good number of Americans today, were also unhappy about their fate. And they nurtured a similar fantasy of leaving all their troubles behind. We know this because the maha kalpa idea turns up in so many different texts across the Buddhist world. The conflagration was a popular belief and one that remains popular even now. Yet Buddhism counters the impulse to escape by showing its ultimate absurdity. When the Diamond Sutra and Lotus Sutra appear to express a kind nervousness about the coming kalpa fire, they're really just playing along with us, encouraging our escapist dreams. But after we've had a lot of horrifying fun, the sutras tell us what we may not want to hear: change will always bring us more of the same. In the next moment, or the next universe, the bills will be back, the stress, and the kids who still won't pick up their dirty clothes. Subhuti and the other bodhisattvas know that nothing can be gained when all we've done is trade this world for another one.

In particular, those two sutras want us to see that hoping for a better life in some other world is like trying to get off a stationary bike by pedaling faster and faster. If we don't like our job, we can get another one. We can move to another state, lose twenty pounds, grow a mustache and a beard or shave both of them off. But every time we try to separate ourselves from the here and now, our dissatisfaction seems to follow us like a shadow underfoot. Sooner or later, it will always come back, if not in the old form, then as something else. Instead of taking us to a better place, trying to fly away creates more suffering, and it brings about this result because the problem really isn't what we think. The problem isn't getting stuck—with the bills, the job, the crazy kids. The problem is wanting to escape.

When we fix our minds on the universe as it deliciously goes up in flames, we're really saying it's a bad place to be, not at all the one we wanted. But the Diamond and Lotus Sutras both suggest that this outlook is a big mistake. The cosmos, they say, is actually one enormous system working day and night to liberate us from our suffering. And sooner or later we'll understand, even if we go through innumerable lives wishing we were somewhere else. Sooner or later our perspective will change, and then our unhappiness will fall away. Even though Daizui's words—being Zen—are saturated with ambiguity, the point of the story in which he appears is pretty much the same as this. What has to perish is the dream of escape, and once that's dissolved it won't matter if the kalpa fire burns the world to ashes or not.

THE TIMELESS IN THE MIDST OF TIME

The Bible isn't just another sacred book. As I've said, it's a book about time as well. And it teaches us that time is a long, winding road that will lead us to a better place in the end. Until we arrive we're "strangers in a strange land," wanderers like the children of Israel during their time in the wilderness.[84] The proper attitude is to keep your bags packed, as this passage from Luke suggests:

> As they were walking along the road, a man said to [Jesus], "I will follow you wherever you go." Jesus replied, "Foxes have holes and birds of the air have nests, but the Son of Man has no place to lay his head." [Jesus] said to another man, "Follow me." But the man replied, "Lord, first let me go and bury my father." Jesus said to him, "Let the dead bury their own dead, but you [should] go and proclaim the kingdom of God." Still another said, "I will follow you, Lord; but first let me go back and say good-bye to my family." Jesus replied, "No one who puts his hand to the plow and looks back is fit for service in the kingdom of God."[85]

Here Jesus declares his indifference to the preoccupations of this world. To bury your father or to say goodbye is to still behave as though life on earth mattered. For Jesus in the Gospel of Luke, it didn't. God's Kingdom would arrive with the Apocalypse, and that event was already well on its way. Service to God's Kingdom meant giving up everything about this fleeting world. As Jesus teaches in the passage above, you can't so much as take a backward glance. Turn your eyes to the future and begin to walk.

But what about the Buddhist view? When people think of the Buddha's life, they may not connect it to history. Yet the story of the Buddha's enlightenment is all about the proper way to live with time.

At the start of his search for enlightenment the young man later called the Buddha chose to set out on the ancient Indian path of the forest-dwelling holy men or rishis. Leaving behind the wealth and security of the palace where he was born, Siddhartha Gautama became a wandering ascetic. He owned nothing and begged for the little that he ate, sleeping in graveyards and devoting the day to the deepest meditation. Yet in spite of all his efforts, including extreme fasts that left him nearly dead, Siddhartha could find no solution to the problem of suffering, which he saw everywhere he turned.

Discouraged and starving, he finally left his five companions, wandering to a little village nearby. There a kindly peasant girl, moved by pity at his wretched state, gave him a meal of milk and rice. Strengthened by this simple food, Siddhartha resolved to try one more time, and seating himself under a pipal tree, he descended again into the depths of concentration. It was then that he experienced enlightenment.

In the Bible when the Holy Spirit comes, it can descend in many different ways—like a chariot of fire or a white dove of peace—but it always reaffirms the chosen person's role in the forward motion of history. When the Buddha described his enlightenment, he struck a very different note. For the most part, he said what enlightenment was *not*. "My deliverance is unshakable," he declared, "This is my last birth. Now there is no renewal of being."[86] He was also supposed to have recited this *gatha* or enlightenment poem:

Through many births
I have wandered on and on,

Searching for, but never finding,
The builder of [this] house....
House-builder, you are seen!
You will not build a house again!
All the rafters are broken,
The ridgepole destroyed;
The mind, gone to the Unconstructed,
Has reached the end of craving.[87]

No renewal of being, nothing left to desire—this is the opposite of "I'll Fly Away."

If the Christian Apocalypse is an "uncovering"of God's grand design, the Buddha's enlightenment uncovers something else—the timeless, the eternal, in the midst of time, which is here called "the Unconstructed."

After his enlightenment, the Buddha continued to eat and sleep, walk and talk, but he no longer lived psychologically in a future-directed world where people believe in gain and loss, success and failure, fame and infamy, youth and old age, victory and defeat. His existence was no longer moving toward any better state at all, and nothing he encountered could give rise any more to anger, fear, and delusion.

The Buddha ceased to belong to any tribe, any country, any civilization—not even to himself. Nor did he believe any longer that politics, learning, reputation, art, wealth, or sensual pleasure could make any fundamental change in his condition. The passing away of the heavens and the earth could not have brought about a change in his life more complete than the one that had happened already.

The Sangha of the Buddha's early followers might appear to have formed something much like the early Christian church, which it preceded by about five hundred years. Both were monastic communities of men and women who had walked away from their families and friends. Many early Christians, however, were convinced the world was soon coming to an end. As Jesus promised his followers, it would end before the youngest of them had died. No similar conviction took root in the Sangha because they knew that, for the Buddha, in a sense, the End had already taken place. Liberation wasn't waiting at some future date. Instead, a timeless here and now some-how existed in the midst of time. The Buddha discovered this timelessness, and he taught that it was accessible to anyone at every moment.

THE PURE PRESENCE OF NIRVANA

The West's response to the problem of suffering has been to destroy and remake the world again and again with tremendous energy and imagina-tion. We're driven by a sense of purpose that has the force of a divine com-mand. A recent bestseller by the evangelist Rick Warren is aptly entitled *The Purpose Driven Life*.[88] Every day becomes an Apocalypse—a small Apoc-alypse that we ourselves control. We say to that mountain, "Be moved," and then our bulldozers and caterpillars move it.[89] What emerges from the ruins of the mountain is a world remade by our desires, which we imagine to be God's own. But of course our desires have no end, so the mountain is replaced by a parking lot, and then by a housing development, then a strip mall, and then a factory. This process seems likely to continue until the last quart of gasoline is gone and we'll have to find something else to fuel our dreams.

But the experience of enlightenment is transformative in a way that makes an Apocalypse unnecessary. The Buddha's mind had become "puri-fied, bright, unblemished, rid of imperfection, malleable…and attuned to imperturbability." And with such a mind he could see the world with-out hoping for anything else:

> Just as if there were a lake in a mountain recess, clear, limpid, and undisturbed, so that man with good sight standing on the bank could see shells, gravel, and pebbles, and also shoals of fish swim-ming about and resting, he might think: "There is this lake, clear, limpid, and undisturbed, and there are these shells, gravel, and pebbles, and also these shoals of fish swimming about and rest-ing." So too, [an enlightened person] understands [the moment] as it actually is.[90]

Buddhist tradition has a word for this state—it's called *Tathata* or Thusness. Instead of destroying and remaking the world, the Buddhist approach is to give up on our false ideas about how things should be, which are always less true than reality, the pure presence of this moment. This is the real meaning of the Buddhist word *nirvana*, which is often said to refer to the act of "blowing out," as of a flame. What gets blown out in enlightenment is not life on earth, as Western scholars used to think, but our fears and projections. Created to protect us from suffering, these fears and projections eventually make it impossible to see things as they are.

In the Indian and Tibetan traditions, artworks often show the Buddha seated in a pose that is known as the *bhumi mudra*, "earth witnessing." He is said to have assumed this posture after fending off visions of sensuous pleasure sent by Mara—the mythical personification of samsara—who was trying to prevent his enlightenment. These temptations might be understood as the final remnants of the Buddha's search for a better world—the impulse that lies at the root of all desire, which always seeks its object somewhere else. And so when the Buddha had at last broken through, he adopted the earth witnessing pose, with his palm raised to signal he was teaching while his other hand touched the earth. "This earth is the witness to my enlightenment," he announced, "I have solved the problem of suffering." The sign of his enlightenment, in other words, was his unconditional embrace of this world exactly as it is.

This embrace is the very opposite of Apocalyptic thinking, which stimulates desire in a way that creates further suffering. Remember the God of Genesis, angry and hurt when the world he made takes an unexpected turn. As human beings we have even less control than God, and so our life becomes a kind of lottery. The next number might be the winning one; the next day could bring the fulfillment of our dreams. The *Blue Cliff Record*, a key Zen text, compares this hope to a starving man waiting for a rabbit to crash into a stump so he can cook it for dinner. If he continues to wait expectantly, the man will surely die.[91] And while he is waiting for an event that might never take place at all, a tree could be dropping fruit a few feet away.

One way to understand the Buddha's enlightenment is to say that he *transcended change itself*. We could almost say that he discovered a permanence above the vagaries of earthly life and outside the twists and turns of history. But that understanding wouldn't be quite right. The pure presence of the moment isn't somewhere else—it isn't, say, on a higher plane. There's no unchanging essence or permanent being. Instead the timeless exists in the midst of time. There aren't two realities, a conditioned realm that exists in time and an unconditioned realm that exists somewhere else. Instead, there are two perspectives on the here and now, one enlightened and the other not enlightened yet. For someone in enlightened mind, all the numbers in the lottery become the same. There's no hoping for a specific one. In fact, hope itself becomes irrelevant.

This is the attitude the Buddha recommends in the final lines of the Diamond Sutra:

> So you should see…all of the fleeting world:
> A star at dawn, a bubble in a stream;
> A flash of lightning in a summer cloud,
> A flickering lamp, a phantom, and a dream.[92]

At first, the Buddha's declaration might sound a bit like the passage in the Bible where Jesus says to lay up your treasure in heaven, not on earth.[93] But Jesus's point is that a better life awaits us somewhere else at another time. By contrast, the Buddha sees exactly this hope as the source of all our suffering. The person who awakens at last understands that time can never lead us to the end of time. The flow of transformation will never stop. But when we've ceased trying to arrest the flow or make it go in the direction we want, the character of our awareness will change and this world will become a very different place.

SEEING THINGS AS THEY REALLY ARE

The first Westerners who encountered this view dismissed it as a kind of Oriental fatalism. Lacking the background that would help them make sense of such very strange ideas, they reached for the closest equivalents in their own experience: giving up, giving in, losing hope. These observers thought that the Buddhists had made a cult of detachment and resignation, and this impression grew even stronger when they heard Buddhists talk about cessation, emptiness, and nothingness. The Westerners saw themselves as men of destiny, boldly shaping the world according to their wills, and they considered the Buddha's teachings sickly and weak. As the German philosopher Friedrich Nietzsche wrote in a famous passage, "Buddhism is a religion for *late* men, for gracious and gentle races that have become overly spiritual and excessively susceptible to pain."[94]

Some observers even today imagine meditation as self-absorbed and world-evading. A person on the cushion appears to sink into a private solitude, ignoring everything around him. It looks like an extreme form of tuning out. But this interpretation depends, once again, on the hidden architecture of our thought.

Almost from its start the West has believed that true knowledge comes from our ability to find a single, permanent truth in the midst of differing perspectives. Many people might observe the same event, but the real version will be the one that factors out the variations in their accounts. Today we call this method "objectivity."

But what if all the perspectives are real, and the differences are actually the product of change in a complex universe? The differing perspectives aren't mistakes, but come from occupying different points of view that have arisen through change itself. The Western idea of truth insists that we suppress these differences, acting as though only one can be real. We could call this Apocalyptic thinking on the scale of individual events. For us, the universe is going down one road. Whatever deviates has lost its way.

But we might say the Buddha started with complexity. For him, choosing just a single version of events would have meant ignoring what is in fact the most obvious feature of our lived experience—the coexistence of different points of view, not only within society but even within ourselves. His method was to watch the whole panoply with a calm, impartial mind. He treated all perspectives in much the same way, and didn't try to choose any one of them as right. To the Western eye this might look like an escape, a failure to make the crucial cut that the search for truth requires. But in Zen we'd see it as the most precise and honest means of viewing a complex reality.

The architecture of Western thought leaves us unprepared for what happened when the Buddha used this method. As he watched his own perspectives come and go, gradually concept-formation fell away, followed by sensation, the awareness of time, the awareness of space, even the awareness of being aware. Absolutely nothing remained. But it was here that he made his great discovery. This nothingness was completely different from what most of us might anticipate—a dead void or blank negation. Nothingness was like the sea itself, and out of it everything arose, including even the Buddha.

The Zen master Lin-chi describes it this way: "It has no fixed form; it penetrates all the ten directions. In the eye we call it sight; in the ear we call it hearing; in the nose it detects odors, in the mouth it speaks discourse; in the hand it grasps, in the feet it runs along."[95]

To Western ears, encountering nothingness might sound like the worst calamity that could befall anyone. Nothingness, we think, is a kind of death. The idea that nothingness could be positive seems like a contradiction or a paradox. The ancient Greeks knew about nothingness—indeed, it's what the word "chaos" meant. But after that, the West ran away from the idea.[96] Only now are we in a position to grasp what the Buddha had in mind, thanks largely to the work of physicists. These physicists have told us that the universe sprang out of nothingness with the Big Bang. More recently they've suggested that the Big Bang might have been just one of a series of events, potentially infinite in number.[97] Many physicists now accept the view that when we lump together all the forces of the universe, they cancel one another out.[98] And so the universe (or universes) may have come into existence through a basic "instability" in nothingness itself.

The Buddha wasn't a physicist and he didn't employ the method of physics, but his enlightenment enabled him to see existence in a radically different way. Instead of discovering a permanent self as the center of his consciousness, he directly experienced his own consciousness as arising out of nothing. To say, however, that there's no self at all would be a misunderstanding, and the Buddha never actually made such a claim. On the basis of his enlightenment, he concluded there was no such thing as a permanent self existing independently of everything else. The self and the world really do exist, at least temporarily. The two are inseparable and they arise at the same time. Once the Buddha had this insight, his status as an individual was forever changed. He saw himself as a wave on the ocean of waves, with an existence that was real but conditional. Out of the ocean wave after wave emerges, moving forward strongly for a time, and then finally returning to the sea from which they have never really been apart.

After his enlightenment the Buddha calmly watched everything arising and passing away—two aspects of a single process that goes on forever in a cosmos operating like any other complex, self-organizing system. To ask who is running this whole show is like asking who decided on the patterns made by the waves on the ocean's surface. The wind, the water temperature, the contours of the shore and the ocean floor's topography all give the waves their intelligence. And "intelligence" is not a metaphor, at least from the standpoint of enlightenment. From the vantage point of his awakened mind the Buddha saw clearly that everything without exception is alive. The boundaries between ourselves and others, between mine and yours and even between the animate and inanimate, these are also merely fantasies. Everything participates in one great life.

NOTHINGNESS AND COMPASSION

People have sometimes misunderstood how enlightenment relates to our actions in the everyday world. Our standard image of the Eastern sage is the cartoon of a bearded man hidden away on a remote mountaintop. The assumption is that any person who has moved so far beyond ordinary consciousness would probably regard human suffering with a serene indifference. If the Buddha has passed through the door that separates earthly time from eternity, why should he look back at the rest of us?

Something about the Buddha's story might seem reminiscent of Eucherius in fourth-century France. Anyone who reads the Pali sutras might conclude there's a whole lot of world-despising going on. After all, the Buddha's quest started with the horror he felt when he came face to face with sickness, old age, and death. He saw suffering as the basic fact of our existence in this world:

Wife and children, men and women slaves, goats and sheep, fowl and pigs, elephants, cattle, horses, and mares, gold and silver: these acquisitions are subject to birth, aging, sickness, and death: to sorrow and defilement; and one who is tied to these things, infatuated with them, and utterly absorbed in them, being himself subject to birth…to sorrow and defilement, seeks what is also subject to birth…to sorrow and defilement.[99]

The Buddha became what is known in his tradition as a "home-leaver" or wandering monk. Today we might say with some embarrassment that he deserted his wife and his infant son. He even abandoned the noble throne his father had begged him to assume. The Buddha condemned the world and left it behind—that much seems beyond dispute.

Yet if we look again at the passage above, a few details will complicate this view. Wives and children are called "acquisitions." And what about the phrase "men and women slaves"? If you were raised in such a society, and if you hadn't heard of feminism or learned the words, "all men were created equal," you might suspect that your society was somehow wrong, but you wouldn't know why you felt that way.

Of course the Buddha could have swallowed his doubts. He could have made an effort to fit in and get along. But instead he left and tried to find out what was real. Perhaps at the moment of his home-leaving he might have thought that he had indeed turned his back on the world and its distress, but that's not at all where he eventually wound up.

Like every other human experience, enlightenment is subject to a range of interpretations. Even Buddhist masters sometimes disagree about some crucial details. Yet most people who have gone through the experience, and there have been tens of thousands of them, describe it in remarkably similar ways. To the person caught up in the event, enlightenment can seem like returning to the Source—not only the place where the world comes to an end but also where it all begins. Some people cry, some laugh, and some laugh and cry at the same time. The Buddha is supposed to have sat motionless for seven days. Among his successors over the centuries, the peak experience can end a little sooner.

Perhaps the most surprising aspect of enlightenment is its emotional resonance. Although the Buddha said that the medium of language couldn't do justice to the complexity of the experience of waking up, when he tried to describe it he often used words like "beautiful" and "joyous." But enlightenment might be best described by the word "compassion." To reach the nothingness at the heart of life is to feel a deep connection to everything.

The Buddha's awakening experience didn't leave him up on the mountaintop. In fact, it took him back to earth in the most literal sense. One important detail about the Buddha's story is what happened after his awakening. As his seven days drew to a close, a surprising insight came to him. At first he thought that his awakening was just too strange to convey to anyone: "This Dhamma that I have attained is profound, hard to see and hard to understand.... If I were [to try] to teach the Dhamma, others would not understand me." But in the moment following this thought, the Brahma Sahampati, a god from an abode between the heavens and the earth, appeared before the Buddha and implored, "The world will be lost, the world will perish, since the mind of the Tathagata, accomplished and fully enlightened, inclines to inaction rather than to teaching the Dhamma.... [Let] the Blessed One teach the Dhamma.... There are beings with little dust in their eyes who...will understand."[100]

Like the stories in the Bible, the accounts of the Buddha's enlightenment contain many mythological elements. Rather than seeing Sahampati as a god or "*brahma*," we today might say that he represents an aspect of the Buddha's own awareness, the part that feels compassion for others. The important point about the story—the one that often passes unnoticed—is that the experience of enlightenment brought the Buddha face to face again with the reality of suffering, the suffering of all sentient beings.

Instead of saying, as tradition does, that his enlightenment came to an end after a period of seven days, we might think of that time as the first phase, which was followed by a second one that continued until he died. We might even say the second phase continues to this very day, since the Buddha's followers are still going through the same process and reaching the same liberation.

After the period of awakening, every person will also find the same compassion that the Buddha felt when Sahampati spoke to him. Having turned
away from a world of suffering to reach the timeless source of everything,
each bodhisattva comes back to find a world of time that is—for everyone
else—still turbulent and unhappy. This was the insight Sahampati brought
to the Buddha: you are free, yes, but the suffering of others is still here.
And once the Buddha understood this lesson, he set off to do what Sahampati asked, wandering the world and teaching anyone who would listen,
rich or poor, young or old. Until his death forty-five years later, the Buddha
never stopped. By then, directly and indirectly, he had helped many thousands to wake up.

The Buddha's "noble quest" didn't end with his time under the pipal tree.
Instead, it only started there. Nor did the Buddha transcend the world; he
embraced it by transcending his illusions. Whether or not we ever find ourselves seated on a meditation cushion, any one of us can do the same. When
we embrace the here and now in a way that leads beyond the limits of the
self, we've already started swimming in the same great sea the Buddha
entered long ago. But we can't ride the waves very far without letting go of
something precious. We might imagine it's financial security or the pleas-
ures of the body. But these are actually quite easy to let go. Much harder
to give up is a goal that seems lofty and compelling. That would be the
desire to save the world.

CHAPTER 4:
ONE BODY—THE HIDDEN GROUND
OF LIBERATION

SAVING THE WORLD, OR CONNECTING WITH IT?

Several years ago a story ran on NPR called "Saving the World in Ethiopia: One Child at a Time." The story involved a woman named Jenafir—her last name was never disclosed. As the research coordinator for a medical non-profit, she was responsible for overseeing a team of student volunteers in Ethiopia. Their particular concern was trachoma, a disease that causes certain blindness unless the victim receives early treatment.

Ethiopia sits near the bottom of the list of the poorest countries on earth, with a population that has needed food aid for eight out of the last ten years. Aside from the steady pulse of the reporter's voice, one of the first sounds the microphone picked up was the crying of village children. The eye exam given to those children that day required Jenafir to turn back each child's lid before swabbing the moist interior, an unpleasant procedure even with adults. The report concluded at the long day's end, with Jenafir in her tiny room sorting through test tubes on the floor.[101]

Who wouldn't be inspired by this account? Here was a young American whose sacrifice will leave the world a better place—a woman dedicated, as the title said, to saving the world one child at a time. And the children there clearly needed to be saved—poor, dirty, ill, and without schooling, like millions of other Ethiopians.

A story like this makes a powerful case for the world-changing attitude of the West. When Hegel looked at places like Africa, it seemed to confirm everything he'd argued for. In Africa history had yet to start—history in the

Hegelian sense, as mankind's journey from utter misery to the fulfillment of its maximum potential.[102]

But one moment in the story didn't fit. The most important moment in the whole account, and the one most easily overlooked, was when Jenafir finally had her say. In a few quiet words she seemed to contradict everything the story was written to suggest: "I don't think of myself as saving the world. I think of myself as connecting with the world as it is right now."

It's impossible to know how many listeners noticed this moment of dissonance. Connecting with the world and saving it aren't the same at all. Saving the world is an idea that reaches back to Genesis. Every time that human sinfulness would provoke God into violent retribution once again, heroes would arise to stay his hand. The Book of Revelation takes this logic one more step, making destruction itself the means of the world's deliverance.

"Connecting" implies a different way of interacting with reality, but it's one our culture doesn't really understand. To Western ears it sounds rather trivial or vague. But maybe there's something more to it than that.

THE PROBLEM OF THE TEN DIRECTIONS

When we look at a place like Ethiopia nothing could seem more obvious than our obligation to save the world. If we don't act in Ethiopia, what on earth could ever induce us to try? But saving the world in Ethiopia assumes we can know the direction it should take. Will the Ethiopians be better off if they exchange their way of life for ours—their starvation for our obesity, their oxcarts for our polluting cars and trucks, their failing farms for our agribusinesses, which are likely to drive millions into urban slums? No one would argue with treating eye disease, but do we really know what's best for everyone, or even for ourselves? Do we really know how to set things right?

In Zen there a story called "Kempo's One Road." A monk says to Master Kempo, "I have heard that in every direction you'll see Holy Ones, yet only a single road leads to Nirvana."[103] That's exactly our predicament today— not just in Ethiopia but here in the U.S., and everywhere else on the planet as well. We're confused because we live in a universe where North and

South, East and West aren't absolute. What we call "up" is only up from one point of view. "Left" is only left if you're turned a certain way. Every change of angle generates a completely different perspective. This isn't simply a semantic game—some of the bitterest conflicts today have started over differences of just this kind.

Maybe we each have to choose our own road. But even when we've chosen only for ourselves, things never follow our careful plans. We can't know where we're going until we've gone, and then, when we look back, we're sure to find that everything seems different from where we now stand.

Trying to save Ethiopia could improve the situation on the ground, but it could also make things much, much worse. The country could wind up like Norway or Sweden, frugal, well-governed, and literate. Or it could end as a nightmare state with businessmen in suits but also AK-47s, the internet and the heroin trade, universities and prostitution on the streets. We can observe such disasters today on every continent. Indeed, the U.S. has had a hand in creating some of them.

As the koan puts it, "Holy Ones in ten directions." Everywhere we've looked for the last two hundred years, we thought we had a glimpse of our future paradise, but then as we got closer, it turned into a hell. We ended dysentery in Country X when we shipped in the newest wonder drugs. The babies stopped dying and the future looked bright. Then the population numbers went through the roof, sparking ethnic violence and a civil war. Now the schools are rubble and the babies have grown into gangs patrolling the streets with guns.

We wanted to abolish inequality. We declared, "All men are equal," and the crowds cheered in the streets. But the children of oppression woke up from their sleep, hungry for the wealth their parents wanted more than they ever wanted democracy. Now money has become everything, and to obtain it the strong fight against the weak, the young against the old, the rural villagers against the city folk, and the rich against everybody else.

So far, each road that mankind has walked has ended up in much the same disappointing way. Each road has led us down a cul-de-sac. Yet the sutras still teach, "Nirvana lies straight ahead." It's obvious that we need to act—but how can we act in each particular case, when we really can't tell up from down? There's no solid ground on which to stand, yet somehow we need to plant both feet and walk.

When the monk asks Kempo which road he should take, Kempo raises his staff and draws a line in the thin air, "Here it is," he says, with total confidence. What could Kempo's secret be? How can he declare with such confidence that *this* is the proper way to go when all lines we draw are really drawn in the air? Perhaps if we don't know the way to go, that's because our way of knowing is deeply flawed.

USELESS WISDOM

Let's say that after turning off NPR, you open the covers of your new book, an anthology of classic Buddhist texts. As you flip the pages, your eyes come to rest on the Buddha's conversation with his follower, the bodhisattva Manjushri:

> Manjushri: How can one speak of the qualities or advantages of a perfect wisdom which is incapable of doing anything, neither raises up nor destroys anything, neither accepts nor rejects…is powerless to act and not at all busy….
>
> [The Buddha]: It is called "perfect wisdom" because…it is calmly quiet from the very beginning, because there is no escape, there is nothing to be done.[104]

Mahayana Buddhists revere this dialog as one of the most sublime expressions of the truth. In *The Perfection of Wisdom in 700 Lines*, the Buddha says that no road actually exists. As long as we believe in change of any kind, our minds remain fundamentally deceived. To think in terms of improvement and decline, increase and decrease, gain and loss, birth and death, is to impose on reality qualities it simply doesn't have. When we do this, the motive is always fear, and fear generates a separation between ourselves and everything around us.

Past and future are illusory, the Buddha says; even when we speak about the here and now we risk getting caught in that same trap. He adds that when we look with an awakened mind, every moment will appear exactly the same. It will always have "one taste" and nothing more.[105]

There's something intriguing about this argument, and it's had an enormous effect on the lives of many millions of people. The sutra belongs to a family of texts composed about six or seven hundred years after the Buddha died. These texts transformed the way his followers understood both his enlightenment and their own everyday lives.

The ideas in the sutra have a definite appeal. We'd all like a break from so much busy-ness. We all want to enjoy a little quiet time. "Calmly quiet from the very beginning" sounds good. If that's the essence of the Buddha's teaching, then it's very wise advice indeed. But what if the Buddha means something more? He doesn't just say that we should take a break. He actually says there is "nothing to be done." He says that perfect wisdom is powerless. It doesn't destroy, it doesn't build. It's incapable of doing anything. We'd all like to get off the road for a while, but "no road" is a disturbing idea.

As Manjushri asks, What's the good of that?

It's troubling to think that the sutra implies that we shouldn't try to make the world a better place. The words "nothing to be done" seem to suggest there's no point in flying to Africa to provide medicine for the children there. Instead, the greatest wisdom would appear to lie in letting events run their natural course. Needless to say, this cuts against our Western grain. In the early days of Christianity, the Apostle Paul taught that we should "Fight the good fight."[106] Everybody has to do their part. The rich, Paul said, have obligations to the poor, the masters obligations to their slaves. But here the Buddha seems to preach passivity—calmly going with the flow.

If that's what the Buddha means, then the Apostle Paul wins the argument hands down. We can't turn our backs on Ethiopia in order to preserve our peace of mind. But there may be more in play than this simple choice.

There is, after all, the story of Sahampati, who implored the Buddha to come to the aid of a suffering humanity. Didn't the Buddha work unceasingly for almost fifty years, trying to help everyone who crossed his path? Maybe there's something in the Buddha's words we've missed, something we didn't fully grasp. Is the Buddha telling us not to act? Or are his words meant to help us understand what true liberation might involve?

THE HIDDEN GROUND OF LIBERATION

Saving the world is based on the idea that something we do might cause a fundamental change. If we can only find the one right road, it will take us all the way to paradise. But what if paradise is already here, just not the form we were raised to expect?

Think about your own experience. Late one morning you set out for a drive, and then, after an hour, you go down a road you've never traveled before. You take a turn and find yourself staring straight ahead at a field of wildflowers in late summer bloom. The sky overhead is clear and bright blue, the air is warm, and all around the cicadas are humming. Across the field some grazing horses look at you, swishing their tails to keep away the flies until they go back to the work of chewing grass. You leave the car and walk across the field to the shade of an ancient spreading oak. Then, with your back pressed again the trunk, you look out at a whole horizon filled with fields and trees, and behind them, a row of soft, green hills.

Earlier that day you were very tense—worried by the problems at your job. But now all those worries seem to fade away. Gradually the muscles of your face relax, and you can feel your shoulders slowly loosening. As you sit staring at the summer fields, the thoughts that you couldn't put down before, thoughts you kept turning over in your mind, appear to have vanished beyond recall. The mental screen behind your eyes has suddenly gone blank, and now what you see is simply all you know, all that's going on in your head. As you keep watching you begin to feel as though you're growing empty or dispersed. In some way you don't even want to understand, the fields, the insects, and the slow-moving clouds have become a part of you. For some period, maybe long, maybe short, time itself seems to disappear, and even though the insects are deafening, you feel as though a silence has descended on the scene. Here there is really "nothing to be done." Nothing can be added, nothing taken away.

Everybody's had an experience like this, and some would say that moments of this kind are the ones that make life worth living. And yet if I asked you to explain where the secret of such moments lies, you might have a hard time answering. Maybe the field was what caused you to relax, but then again you've seen other fields with other flowers, but they didn't put you in the same state of mind. You've sat on the grass countless times before, and you've watched the clouds and heard the cicadas trilling, but when you did, you might have hardly noticed them. Something about the moment had this strange effect, but the more you try to analyze and explain, the more elusive it becomes.

The flowers, the fields, the summer breeze—we know they can produce feelings of well-being and connectedness. But the same experience could occur in a very different setting. At six in the evening you leave your cubicle. You catch the elevator and step out on the street. The noise of the traffic almost seems to explode, and the heat comes down on you like extra gravity. Twenty paces forward and you're covered with sweat, pushed and pulled by the human tide. As you rush along with your head bent down, your world is no bigger than your two shoes shuffling along on the burning cement. But then, all at once, your angle of vision opens up dramatically. Everything seems to become clear and bright. A moment ago your world was one square foot. Now it reaches all the way across the street, taking in the crowds and the buildings that extend upward where they merge with the smoggy sky. Everywhere you turn you seem to feel a sense of being part of something bigger than yourself.

A moment like this could happen in a country field, or it could happen in the middle of a city. You could be staring at a pothole in the road. Or, it could take place while you're making love. It's happened to people while they're rotting in jail, and while they're awaiting execution. The common element is the feeling of connection, of being at ease and at home in the world. The fact that it can happen almost anywhere suggests that the cause isn't what we might assume. The trees and the grass swaying in the breeze or the throng pressing forward in the steaming heat—these were elements of the experience, but we really can't say they were the cause. The change can take place in so many different ways because the cause was something in ourselves, some basic shift in the way we perceive.

Was it real or was it just a dream? As soon as we go back to our ordinary minds, the whole experience might appear to melt away. We might even wonder if it ever took place. Maybe we were having a hallucination, or maybe we were simply deceiving ourselves. But it's possible to reach the opposite conclusion: maybe what we found is the reality, while that other world is the illusion. It's possible the wholeness has been there all the time, only hidden in a way we still don't understand.

A thousand years ago in many Chinese temples, you could see large, majestic statues of Kwan-yin, the bodhisattva of compassion. Kwan-yin's name means that she hears the cries of all those who are suffering. She's the one who comforts them in their misery. But the statues might not look as you'd expect. Kwan-yin isn't weeping for the multitudes, nor does her expression show signs of urgency. Instead, her brow is clear, her face is soft and round. Her eyes are half closed in serenity and her lips are curled in the beginnings of a smile. Her body isn't tightly clenched, her clothes dark and worn. Every gesture shows that she's completely relaxed. Often she's depicted with a slender leg pulled up, her right arm resting gently on her knee, while the other leg dangles loosely toward the floor. And finally, she's dressed in the most sumptuous clothes, brilliant reds and pearlescent greens, and all adorned with precious gems and jewelry.[107]

The statues send a powerful message. Connection is the answer to our suffering. When we've become a part of something bigger than ourselves, when we've embraced the fundamental unity, the problem of suffering will disappear. We keep thinking that if we try hard enough, the puzzle of the ten directions can be solved. Then we'll know for certain which road we should take. But maybe certain knowledge isn't what we really need in a complex universe where anything might happen. The search for the road that will change everything—this is the cause of suffering, not the cure. Heaven itself is always here right now. That unity can never be diminished or destroyed. All that we need to do is reconnect.

But how does connection actually happen? Kwan-yin's face is calm and bright, but she doesn't tell us how to find her indestructible serenity. We've all had those moments when the boundaries fall away and we feel connected to everything, but strangely, they don't happen at our command. You might go back on another day to your field of summer flowers and ancient trees, but you'll wait in vain for the feeling to return. You can walk the city street a hundred times, but the world would still be your two shoes again. Just as we can't say why the special moments come, we can't explain why they go away and why they don't return when we want them to.

The fact that they don't happen at our command might hold the key we're looking for. Maybe the experience of unity starts from somewhere deeper in ourselves, deeper than the mind that exercises control. Indeed, it's the disappearance of control that somehow seems to bring about the crucial change.

Perhaps the way we look at things is upside down. Our ordinary mind, the one that thinks and plans, might not be doing what we've always assumed. When we think, we're trying to make the world more whole—more coherent, logical, and complete. But actually the world the thinking mind has made is riddled with blank spaces and contradictions.

Every day most of us drive a car, and yet we really haven't any clue how it works. Sometimes we lift the hood to check the oil, but beyond the cabin where we sit, most of it's a big blank area we're quite happy to leave unexplored. From the faucet in the kitchen, water somehow comes, but by mechanisms none of us can explain, unless we're plumbers or hydraulic engineers. Behind the faucet—who knows what might go on there? It's something that we'll never have to care about until there's a puddle on the floor.

Thinking, we believe, makes our world more complete, but our lives are really held together with tape. Parents want their children to do just what they say, and yet they're also desperate to instill qualities like independence and playfulness. Voters are outraged by a government that's become a haven for liars and crooks, and yet they're still convinced that it's the very best on earth. Even philosophers and scientists, who pride themselves on their rationality, live in a mental house that's missing walls, with pipes protruding from the floor and stairways leading into empty space.

The world of consciousness is really like that, and when we look too closely we become distressed. Then we have the problem of the multiple roads and not knowing which of them we should take. The closer we look the more we see the blank spaces and the impossibilities.

So we try to avoid looking closely. In fact, nothing short of an emergency—a Great Depression or a terrorist attack—will jolt most people out of their comfort zone, and perhaps even these might not do it.

FLOATING ON THE OCEAN OF ENLIGHTENED MIND

We always believe we glimpse the holy ones ahead. And yet among the ten directions we can never know which will prove to be the one we should have selected. Somehow our mental maps don't correspond to a complex reality.

But let's say you're on the ocean far from the land, so far that it's become impossible to tell where your little boat is heading. Your only hope is to find a reference point now that the shore is out of sight. Maybe you try to keep your eye on the sun or you look for fixed stars when the sun goes down. But what if clouds obscure the evening sky? Once the stars have begun to disappear you find yourself losing hope until you turn and spot something floating there, right beside the boat. Someone's left a buoy to guide future sailors. Above it is a sign that says "Sail this way" over an arrow pointed straight ahead. After a while you find another buoy, with another arrow and another sign.

This is our situation in a universe as vast and ever-changing as the sea. We navigate by relying on those signs, which we call "words" and "ideas." Without those fixed points we'd feel totally lost and we'd begin to drift despondently. Long ago—perhaps a hundred thousand years—the invention of those buoys saved our collective lives. But at that happy moment in our prehistory, we were so relieved that we overlooked one small but vitally important detail: the buoys were floating freely too.

The surface of the ocean is in constant flux, but so are words and ideas. Like us, they're born, they grow old, and they die.[108] Each year a small army of lexicographers—the men and women who compile dictionaries—has to remove the corpses of old words that no one uses any more. Old words go out, new words get added in. As for ideas, they're exactly the same—subject to continuous change. With ideas, there are always fads and trends. There are booms, bubbles, and collapses too.

The conscious mind's reliance on words and ideas has made the world a better place in countless ways. We've used them to build schools and hospitals. We've passed wise laws and established governments, cured diseases and prolonged human life. We've written brilliant works of literary art, and extended human knowledge so far and fast that it's said to double every year.

Yet there's still one thing they cannot do. They can't provide us with the certainty we've lost when the buoys begin to shift. Then, when our words and ideas fail, nothing works properly anymore. The kids go to school, but they don't seem to learn. Patients get ill at the hospital. Governments lock down in paralysis and there's nothing good to watch on TV. We want words and ideas to give us permanence, but gradually the tides of change pull everything apart. Worse yet, when people feel increasingly adrift, they become fearful and dangerous. You'll cling desperately to your little buoy while I cling with growing anxiety to mine. At moments like this, when we want to be saved, we tell ourselves we're trying to save the world.

But words and ideas might not be our only way of navigating. Instead of looking nervously to the sun and stars, or to the buoys as they float away, we can depend on the sea itself.

At our moments of connection with the world, the mind that thinks with words and ideas recedes, and then another kind of intelligence appears. Often, it's like you're in a waking dream. You're fully alert and yet the fear has gone, the fear that haunts your daylight hours, out of view but always there. Now your obstructions have disappeared. Anything and everything are possible.

When the monk Bodhidharma came from India to China, where he taught what later became known as Zen, he brought along with him a single book, the Lankavatara Sutra. It poses the same dilemma that we face today—the dilemma of the multiple roads. If we look at the world with the conscious mind, what we often see is complete disorder: people running madly in every direction, "coming and going on [the surface of the] earth" like wild birds weaving through air in panicked flight.[109] When every certainty seems to melt in thin air, where can we ever hope to plant our feet? But the sutra insists that this state of disorder is actually an illusion. Our conscious minds lead us to believe that we're cast adrift like a little boat buffeted by the enormous waves. But the sutra also says the unconscious mind knows that the sea is what we really are.[110]

What happens in our special moments is that we experience an opening between the conscious mind and this larger unconscious one, the mind that only knows things as a unity. In Zen the word for this opening is *kensho*, "seeing our true nature" or "our true self." What we see is our oneness with the world.

It's certainly true that the conscious mind can become aware of this unity, but the unconscious mind is the source. When we leave home in the morning we don't choose to hear the birds or smell the air. In fact, we can't even choose our thoughts. Like all forms of awareness they arise without conscious decision on our part.

Choiceless awareness is the way. If you go to a Zen center to learn meditation, some kindly person will show how to sit with your spine straight, your legs on the mat, and your hands neatly folded in your lap. If you lean to the left, she will center you again. If you start to crane forward, she will gently push you back. If you keep squirming and sighing heavily, the meditation hall monitor might yell at you, telling you that you're disturbing everyone. Because of this, it's quite possible to think that Zen is all about control and discipline. But this assumption would be a big mistake. Zen is about sitting like Kwan-yin—not in the same posture, that is true, but with the same ease and effortlessness. Zen is about learning how to trust the power of the unconscious mind. We learn how to let that Buddha mind do its work. And when it does, our obstacles begin to disappear.

CARING FOR OUR ONE BODY

In twentieth century Japanese Zen, one of the most respected figures of all was Yamamoto Gempo Roshi, whose family members were forced by poverty to abandon him shortly after his birth. Taken in by a childless couple, he was often beaten by his adoptive father, and drifted into drinking and adolescent crime. Probably he would have continued this way if it hadn't happened that his eyes began to fail just as he was turning twenty-one. Legally blind for the rest of his long life, he spent several years on an extended pilgrimage to Shinto and Buddhist holy sites across Japan. Once he eventually began to practice Zen, progress didn't come easily, and his training as a priest was made even harder because he'd never really learned how to read.[111]

During World War II, when he was in his seventies, Gempo supported the dictatorship, like the vast majority of his countrymen. Almost everybody saw the war as justified—a way to save the world they knew and loved. And even though they faced overwhelming odds, the Japanese believed a better future lay ahead if they were willing to sacrifice themselves for the sake of a greater good. Very few Japanese understood the war's actual complexity, and indeed, very few wanted to. Gempo, sadly, wasn't one of them. Even though he'd given more than fifty years to the cultivation of wisdom through Zen, he also lost his way in the confusion. To criticize the country in the middle of a war was absolutely unthinkable. But when the war had ended, the truth was obvious: loyalty brought ruin and defeat, as well as untold suffering.

What do you do when you learn one day that you're lost amid the ten directions? Where do you turn when you realize that you've failed in the most shameful and egregious way? That was the fate of the postwar Japanese. The tides of change had swept away their certainties. Now, left was right and up was down. But on such occasions something special can occur. A truth more real than our certainties has the chance to manifest itself. There, amid the ruin of his beliefs, monk Gempo seems to have undergone a change. His simple kindness and humility helped many people to accept the fate they'd feared more than anything, the fate of humiliation and defeat. Zen didn't save Gempo from his mistakes. In a complex universe, nothing can do that. But it showed him how to live once he had failed. What he'd had to learn in the hardest way, and what he'd somehow overlooked for so many years, is that we can't fall out of unity. If the Japanese had only understood, it would have made the war unnecessary. And even if the war had gone on, knowing this might have helped people to resist the climate of intimidation.

In the koan "Kempo's One Road," when the monk asks which way to go, the master tells him that he should walk straight ahead. With his staff the master draws a straight line in the air. He doesn't mean that all our judgments will be right, or that if we practice Zen we'll end up like Bill Gates. He doesn't promise that we'll never have regrets, but he wants the monk to understand that success doesn't really liberate, and that failure doesn't mean an eternity in hell. Even in the depths of hell there's only one way out—unifying with the here and now.

Apparently, in Gempo Roshi's later life this became one of his favorite sayings: "In the myriad forms a single body is revealed."[112] When you think about what he went through, that makes perfect sense.

The conscious mind normally assumes that our lives can be enriched by adding what we lack. Or we fear that losing something has the power to detract from our lives in a way we'll never manage to recover from. Generally, the plans we make are based on calculation. One plus one adds up to two. One from four is always three.

But this is not at all the mathematics of life. In reality, nothing can add or subtract. One will never be more or less than one. When we pay attention to the moment as it is, words and ideas begin to fade away until the grasping mind comes to a stop and everything without exception disappears. Then, when there's nothing left to grasp, the world returns in a different form, and we encounter everybody and everything as part of one great life together. In the myriad forms of our existence—as men and women, as young and old, even as rocks and trees—all of us belong to *this*. We can't save the world because no "world" remains, only this connection to everything.

Once we've given up on saving the world, we can replace it with a "solidarity" that goes far beyond that word's conventional meaning. The future will always be a big question mark, and things will get better and worse by turns, forever and ever without end. We can never see the outcome in advance or make events go according to plan. All we have is this single body.

People who have done a great deal of meditation are a lot like those who have lived in one place for a very long time. In different ways they both gain the simplicity of the "one taste" mind. Who they are is all they're ever going to be. Making a statement or making a splash—these have become unimportant and absurd. Everyone around has known them for so long that nothing they can do would cause much surprise. When they go to the dry cleaners or the store, when they walk through the hallways on the job, the real point is simply being present here and now, together with everybody else. For such people, the pleasure of this state—the pleasure of connecting with everyone—has become like drinking from a mountain spring. You don't have to be a Zen master to know how delicious that water really is.

Another kind of master, Louis Armstrong, left behind his expression of the "one taste" mind:

> I see trees of green, red roses too
> I see them bloom for me and you
> And I think to myself what a wonderful world
> I see skies of blue and clouds of white
> The bright blessed day, the dark sacred night
> And I think to myself what a wonderful world
> The colors of the rainbow so pretty in the sky
> Are also on the faces of people going by
> I see friends shaking hands saying how do you do
> They're really saying I love you.[113]

Sometimes we use the word love as it's used here, to describe a mind that has gone beyond likes and dislikes of every kind. The pleasure of others becomes our pleasure too. Their joy becomes our greatest happiness. But of course when we see things in this way, we're leaving out something quite important. Even though the song doesn't raise this point, what about their suffering?

Somebody once asked Master Dogo to explain what the bodhisattva of compassion feels when she uses her thousand arms to help the legions of people who are in need. The bodhisattva of compassion is Kwan-yin, the one represented with such calm and poise by the statues from the T'ang dynasty. When she hears the cries of those who suffer in this world, how does the bodhisattva react? Does her heart break with pity? Does she get mad like the God of Genesis? Does a quiet desperation fill her heart? Dogo told the monk she feels nothing special, like a person half asleep in the night who straightens up her pillow with her hand.[114] This is "one taste" in its active form. The Taoists had a special term for it, wu-wei—to try without trying or to act without regard for conditions or results. "The best are like water," as Lao Tzu said, "Bringing help to all."[115] In Zen we think there's no way out of suffering except to embrace the world exactly as it is, and to embrace it just as naturally as we might adjust our pillow in the night.

Dogo didn't mean we shouldn't try to be of help. In fact, his point was the very opposite. Helping should take place without a moment's thought, and when we hesitate it plainly shows that we're still enmeshed in the conscious mind and selfishness that it perpetuates. But he also meant to make another point as well. If we can't embrace the world in this natural way, then we might cure someone's eyes or dress their wounds, but their suffering—and ours—will still remain.

IS CONNECTING GOOD ENOUGH?

This may be another year when Ethiopians are going to require food aid just to survive. In northeastern Africa and across the Red Sea, the once green hills are drying up as the world gets steadily warmer.

When we look at a problem like climate change, it's hard not to foresee an Apocalypse, yet even now, nothing much is getting done. Among the signers of the Kyoto Protocol, only a few nations have kept to the terms. In most of the countries, emissions have increased, despite the Protocol's modest constraints. Worse yet, some nations simply wouldn't sign, including China, India, and the United States.

If conferences and diplomacy won't work, it stands to reason we should turn directly to the people—just as Al Gore did with *An Inconvenient Truth*. Millions of viewers watched the movie he made, and several billion more might have gone to the "Live Earth" concerts it inspired. But as Gore's detractors were delighted to point out, petroleum powered the planes and cars that got everybody to the stadiums. And the concerts left behind mountains of trash, mostly plastic also made from fossil fuels.

"Live Earth" was a noble effort, not a waste of time. But what has happened as a consequence? True, people tossed their incandescent bulbs. When they could afford it they bought organic food, and some of them went online to do a search for a list of sustainable companies. They sent money to the environmental lobbies and wrote their representative in Washington. All of this will help; but surely not enough. If every business in America could erase its carbon footprint in the coming next year, a global disaster would only be postponed for a little more than century. Even if we do everything we should, most experts think we will be carried along on a wave of climate change already underway.

We're all like the monks in the famous Zen story about Master Nansen and the cat:

> [Master Nansen] saw the monks of the Eastern and Western halls quarreling over a cat. He held up the cat and said: "If you can give an answer, you will save the cat. If not, I will kill it." No one could answer, and Nansen cut the cat in two.[116]

This story centers on an argument between two groups of monks over the temple cat. Finally the argument grew so intense that no one was getting any meditation done, and so Nansen challenged them to say some word that would demonstrate awakened mind. Despite the urgency of the challenge from Nansen—the cat's life and his karma were both at stake—the monks couldn't answer because they remained trapped by indecision. And so, sadly, Nansen cut the cat in half.

Today we can't decide what to do about our "cat"—the failing of our environment. One monk from the Eastern hall wants to try cap-and-trade emissions controls. Another monk from the Western hall disagrees. He worries over the loss of jobs and wants to see the market operate freely. Most of us don't know what we should believe. We listen to the arguments and try to think them through. But the more we listen, the more confused we grow. Should we fail to answer, our cat will surely die, but if Master Nansen were to ask for our advice, who among us would have the confidence to respond with conviction?

James Lovelock, a leading scientist and the author of the *Gaia Hypothesis*, recently wrote that a catastrophe has become unavoidable. Any remedy will come too late. Our paralysis in the face of such a massive threat shows that the problem isn't simply technical. It's not just about coal power plants or cars, the way we grow our food or run the government. Instead, it's a problem with our total way of life—and it seems to call for nothing less than a truly revolutionary change.

But there's more to the story of Nansen and the cat. We learn from the koan that after the event, Nansen's senior student Joshu returned. When Nansen told him about what had transpired, Joshu removed his sandal, placed it on his head, and walked out of the room. Seeing this, Nansen said, "If you had been there, you would have saved the cat."

This response is normally understood to mean that Joshu has attained the effortlessly unified mind that Master Dogo praised—the mind which doesn't try to take the "right" path but connects with the world in an unhesitating way. Unlike the monks, Joshu would have understood that any answer that might have saved the cat would have been appropriate. The most important thing was to try. And yet this explanation still leaves something unresolved. What good does Joshu's action do? What's left, after all, when the cat's already dead?

The paralysis of the world today makes our Apocalyptic paradigms more compelling than they've ever been before. A greener world, a world that won't heat up—if we could only find the collective will, the vision already seems to lie within reach. Perhaps in some corner of the planet there's a mind so brilliant it can tell us how we should proceed. Maybe at this moment there's a Hegel or a Marx drawing up the blueprints for utopia. With such a plan, they could rouse the multitudes.

But doesn't this way of thinking simply reinstate the world-creating/world-destroying attitude that brought us to our impasse now? What if the world has never needed to be saved? What if it is, as the Mahayana teaches, perfect from the very start? Haven't our efforts to save the world actually pushed it to the very edge?

There's something the koan leaves unresolved, and maybe that's because there's something still unclear about reality itself. When we dream of revolutionary change, are we dreaming of a better world, or are we really saying no to the world itself?

CHAPTER 5:
FROM REVOLUTIONARY THINKING
TO AN ECOLOGY OF MIND

When we apply a phrase like "saving the world" to the act of helping others, it draws us back into the Bible's view of time as a road that ends with the events described in the Book of Revelation. But Buddhists for thousands of years have relied on a very different architecture of thought. Just as the Bible has influenced us, so the sutras were the source of countless paradigms that shaped a common understanding of life. The Buddha's teachings on impermanence became a part of the architecture Asian Buddhists used for centuries to make sense of events. For example, in the *Divyavadana*, a collection of Buddhist stories from ancient India, this haunting poem appears:

> All that is accumulated is lost in the end,
> what goes up comes down in the end,
> what comes together comes apart in the end
> and what lives must die in the end.[117]

This poem is like a window that frames the view in a distinctive way. When we look through that window we can plainly see existence as a circle of life and death, a circle that keeps turning forever. Concurrent causes summon each thing into being, but then, "what comes together comes apart."

The circle and the road, the East and the West—today these different architectures both survive, but not exactly on equal terms. Western ideas have gone everywhere, while Buddhist ideas have only recently begun to travel to the West. As a result, when Western writers try to explain Buddhist ways of seeing, they have to rely on the paradigms familiar to their own society.

Of all those paradigms "revolution" may be the most exciting of them all. We might understand the Dharma as a way of "overthrowing" our fundamental ignorance. And enlightenment becomes a kind of revolution too, first inside the self and then in the larger world. Even the Buddha can be described as a revolutionary who set out to overthrow the values of his time and place.

The choice of revolution also reflects our unhappiness with the current state of things. Even though the modern era started out with great optimism and energy, many of the problems we'd hoped to leave behind have now returned, less tractable than ever. And new problems like global warming have emerged, so enormous that the consequences almost seem too terrible to contemplate.

Revolution isn't just another idea. Revolutionary thinking has always been a powerful current in Western thought, starting with the Bible and developing over many centuries. Once the Dharma has become revolutionary, it moves from the margins to a central place in the conversations on contemporary life.

Zen teaches us that reality lies beyond words and ideas. But we still need to use them to communicate, and they always frame our experience in one way or another. That's why we have to think quite carefully about the words and ideas we choose. Like the idea of "saving the world," the idea of "revolution" seems to express something essential about the Buddha's path. But here again we might wind up falling back on the very paradigms we're trying to replace. In this process of translation something can get lost—not only a very different view of time but a different understanding of Buddha's way. As the ancient Buddhist poem observes, "what goes up comes down in the end, what comes together comes apart." Is the Dharma a road to revolutionary change, or does the circle take us somewhere else?

THE DREAM OF REVOLUTION AND THE RUNAWAYS

Revolution is a very powerful dream—a chance to leave the past behind and start the world at Year One again. Few dreams can be more inspiring to anybody trapped beneath history's wheel. Generations of artists and intellectuals have wanted to serve as revolution's high priests, and millions of ordinary citizens have ardently believed the dream and marched hand in hand toward utopia. When the word *revolution* crosses people's lips it has seemed to fly to heaven like the prayer it is:

> Arise, damned of the earth,
> Arise, prisoners of hunger....
> Let us make a blank slate of the past.
> Crowds, slaves, arise, arise!
> The world is changing at the base,
> We are nothing, let's be everything!
> This is the final struggle.[118]

These lines come from "The Internationale," the communist anthem composed in France in 1893. Sixty years after it was written, something like a fourth of all humanity knew the words by heart. Even now the *Communist Manifesto* enjoys an enduring popularity, with at least three different editions in the top thousand books on Amazon.

Revolutions challenging established governments are still a defining feature of modern life, but they aren't the only revolutions that we've seen. For a century it has been commonplace to speak of revolutions in science, health, technology, the arts, and finance. Given our history it's no surprise that Buddhist writers might want to describe the Dharma as revolutionary in some way. Either you're for revolution or you're for backwardness, oppression, and inequality. But the issue might be somewhat more complex than that simple opposition would suggest. There might be another way of viewing change, and other forms of liberation.

In the *Gateless Gate*, an anthology of koans often used in the teaching of Zen, there's a koan that goes like this: "Goso said to his monks, 'Seijo's soul has separated from her being. Which was the real Seijo?'"[119]

The koan refers to a Chinese tale about ill-fated lovers. When she was little Seijo used to play with her cousin Ochu, whom she dearly loved. Adults who saw the children holding hands would say, "There go the old man and wife," as though the two were octogenarians, married for fifty or sixty years. But later, when Seijo had become an adult, her father betrothed her to someone else for the advantage of the family.

In the Confucian culture of China, obedience to parents, "filial piety," was the single most important obligation. Seijo was expected to put aside her feelings for her cousin and wed the man her parents had chosen on her behalf. But try as she might, Seijo couldn't comply, and finally Seijo and Ochu eloped, sailing up the Yangtze River in a small boat. Far away from Seijo's home they found a place to live. There they had two children and enjoyed all the happiness they'd imagined in their dreams. Yet over time Seijo grew despondent because her mind kept turning to her parents, whom she missed, and to her happy memories of childhood. Even though she didn't regret what she'd done, she was filled with nostalgia and a sense of loss. Finally she asked Ochu to take her back so she could see her parents and apologize.

When she arrived in the village once again Seijo was tearful and over-joyed. She wanted to run up to her family home but because she didn't know how she'd be received, she remained in the boat while Ochu went to the compound where he knocked on the courtyard door. Because so many years had passed, when Ochu was let in he had to explain to the parents who he was. He said that even though the two of them ran away, they had returned to apologize and repair the damage.

But Seijo's parents didn't understand at all. "What are you talking about?" they said. "When you left, Seijo's heart was broken. She fell ill, and for all these years, she's been lying in her bed, listless and withdrawn."

When Ochu saw Seijo lying on her bed he was astonished and rushed back to the boat, where Seijo was still waiting. Together they raced to her parents' home and then, when they all went up to Seijo's room, the two Seijos met each other's eyes and suddenly melded into one again.

That's the story on which the koan is based, but what exactly does it mean?

We could say that Seijo and Ochu chose to defy a society that refused to offer them the personal freedoms we take for granted now. The Confucian orthodoxy had become increasingly rigid over time. Under the emperor a miniscule elite lorded over the society, and every Middle Kingdom family was supposed to imitate this order with the eldest male playing the emperor's role. When Seijo and Ochu decided to elope, they became complete outsiders. What they did we might call "revolutionary"—they turned their backs on the status quo and started the world all over again.

As "The Internationale" declares, "Let us make a blank slate of the past." In exile the two lovers were completely free to reinvent their way of life. Indeed, the original story relates that they did so quite successfully. But the story includes some complicating details. Even though the two of them wanted to be free, and even though the freedom they found was genuine, Seijo still felt that she was pulled in two. Leaving the past behind hadn't set her free from the sense that something was missing in her life, and so she and Ochu tried to go home again. But there her contradictions assumed a form she could no longer evade or deny. Her new way of life had brought her happiness and health but left her without her family. The old way left her lifeless on the bed, but gave her the home she was missing.

What takes place after that happens magically. Somehow the contradictions get resolved, but the magical solution explains nothing at all. Instead it forces us to ask ourselves what we would do if we were caught in the same bind, and we had no magic to get out of it. The question is far from hypothetical. Everywhere we turn we come up against contradictions between hopes and realities—between the lives we want to lead and the ones in which we can feel hopelessly trapped. How are we supposed to live in a world where such contradictions tear us apart?

CONTRADICTION AND REVOLUTION IN THE WEST

In the West contradiction has been understood as the product of the Fall. The Bible's first exiles are Adam and Eve, and when they leave their home it's because they've lost a moral contest between right and wrong. In Eden God makes it absolutely clear which foods they could eat and which they should avoid, and as we are told in Genesis, they knowingly defy the instructions God gave. Tempted by the serpent who promises Eve that eating the apple would make her wise like God, she disobeys God's orders and bites into the fruit. Then Adam joins her in the act of defiance. When God returns and finds out what they've done, Adam blames Eve—as well as God himself, for putting her with him in the Garden.[120]

What humans lose in the Fall is moral clarity. As nations and as individuals, all the people in the Bible try to find the proper way to live in their post-Edenic world, but contradictions bar them everywhere they turn. The non-Jews are misled by their false beliefs, and even among the Jews, God's favored few, no leader ever manages to keep the terms of their ancient covenant. God chooses David to rule Israel, and David's son Solomon was renowned for a wisdom without equal. Yet the Bible represents both men as deeply flawed, and they leave behind a legacy that contains the seeds of Israel's decline.

Because of innumerable failures like these, God selects the prophets, special women and men, to serve as his voice among the Jews. Their job is to bring back moral clarity by reporting on events that haven't happened yet but are on the way. The paradigm of prophecy helped to create a view of time that has become ever since an enduring feature of the West. We believe the future already exists. Perhaps we no longer think so consciously, but the paradigm survives in our view of time. And as futurologists and market forecasts show, we also still believe in something like prophecy. Somehow the future is waiting for us, and if we can only get in touch with it, our present contradictions can be resolved.

Christianity took this thinking one step farther. The Jewish Bible seems to say that moral clarity is hard to reach but still attainable. Christians viewed the problem as more severe. Here are the words of the Apostle Paul:

> When I want to do good, evil is right there with me. For in my inner being I delight in God's law; but I see another law at work in the members of my body, waging war against the law of my mind and making me a prisoner of the law of sin at work within my members. What a wretched man I am! Who will rescue me from this body of death?[121]

Paul sees contradiction as the legacy of sin, just like the authors of Genesis. But contradiction is no longer just a result of the bad choices that humanity has made. It's in the very fabric of earthly life. Our hearts pull us in one way, our bodies in another. The result is complete paralysis. In Paul's mind, contradiction is so powerful that none of us can ever hope to break free.

But after his conversion, when Paul looks into his heart, he finds the faith to trust that God will show him what to do. This faith in the future allows him to act with an unshakable confidence. For him, the transformation is revolutionary. It ends his paralysis and lets him set forth as God's warrior, fighting for the good.

Paul took his inner revolution out into the world, challenging an earthly law he saw as corrupt. From Arabia to Turkey, and from Macedonia in northern Greece to Jerusalem, he spoke to local Christian groups, offering advice and encouragement. Eventually, he made his way to Rome, where he was imprisoned and later killed. Amazingly, Paul's revolution won. Less than three centuries after his death, the Empire had adopted Christianity as its official religion.

From that moment onward the future has been the most important verb tense in the West. Even after modern thinkers turned their backs on the religion of Jesus and Paul, their faith in the future remained intact, with results that have been astonishing in both their creativity and their destructiveness.

Looking back over the centuries, we can see everywhere the damage done in the future's name. And now, as the failures keep adding up, the future has begun to look less and less like the utopia of our dreams. Yet the trouble with the future isn't simply that it might turn out in a disappointing way, or that our faith has blinded us to the costs. The trouble is we've never understood time itself. And time is what the Seijo story is all about.

AFTER THE REVOLUTION—ENTER THE TAO

The fact that the Seijo tale comes from old China shows that people then also wanted to get free from the contradictions in their lives. The word "revolution" doesn't turn up in the story, but still the koan tempts us to believe that the future somehow holds the key. Isn't this the lesson of the magical ending? Someday our problems could vanish just like that.

When we remind ourselves that magic isn't real, a sense of frustration might begin to set in. What, if anything, is the koan meant to teach? Maybe there's no way out of any contradiction. Maybe there's no way to ever be free.

But then we start to think about enlightenment. In the future, if we were truly enlightened, we'd know how to extricate ourselves from anything. Then we'd no longer be split in two, and everywhere we turned we'd see a straight road ahead. Of course, we not might be enlightened yet, but if we keep practicing with diligence, at some future time everything will be resolved. The Apostle Paul said it beautifully: "Now we see but a poor reflection as in a mirror; then [in the future] we shall see face to face."[122]

In his famous commentary on the Seijo koan, Master Mumon plays with just these fears and goads us to pursue this very line of thought:

> When [after your enlightenment] you realize what the real is, you will see that we pass from one husk to another like travelers stopping for a night's lodging. But if you do not realize it yet, I earnestly advise you not to rush about wildly. When earth, water, fire, and air suddenly separate, you will be like a crab struggling in boiling water with its seven or eight arms and legs. When that happens, don't say I didn't warn you![123]

The future is our only hope. Unless we find a way out of our divided mind, we will be the crab in boiling water with its legs and arms flailing. Mumon even drags in the kalpa fires to heighten our anxiety. Not only do our lives remain divided now, but when the kalpa fires come, we'll burn for a long time in their hellish flames. Like Paul we might want to cry out desperately, "Who will rescue me from this body of death?"[124]

Every koan is a story that contains a contradiction of some kind—either in plain view or slyly tucked away behind a casual word or phrase. But in Seijo's tale it hits us right between the eyes. And as Mumon understood very well, when we're caught in its grip, we want to fly away. But maybe Mumon's hidden purpose was to show that even if we could indeed fly away—even to another universe—our divided minds will follow us. Perhaps our contradictions can't be solved by looking to the future. Perhaps we need to see the story in a different light. We know there's a Seijo who ran away, and we know there's one who lay sick in her bed. But maybe we're overlooking something obvious. When the master asks "Are they two or are they one?" could he be hinting that both answers are right?

If you ever study philosophy, one of the first lessons you will probably learn is called the law of noncontradiction. The law states that two opposing claims can't be true at once. If A equals B, then we have to reject the opposing proposition: A and B aren't equal. Either something is the case or it's not. Either Seijo will be free or she won't. Either she'll be healthy or she will be ill.

In the West, the noncontradiction law has always been considered unbreakable. And, apparently, in the Buddhist parts of Asia, some logicians have agreed. Not all Buddhists are logicians, though—Zen in particular produces very few. One explanation for this deficit is that the world might actually be more complex than the law allows.

This possibility was noticed long ago by thinkers living in China. Among the greatest of them was Chuang Tzu, a Taoist who strongly influenced Zen. In his writings he gives this account of a legendary fish, "so large its breadth cannot be measured":

> Suddenly [...] it [morphs] into a bird called a P'eng with a back so long there's no way to know where it ends. Only with enormous effort can it rise on huge wings that cover the sky like clouds across the heavens.... When P'eng takes off for the Southern Darkness, the ocean's waves are beaten flat across a thousand miles or more. Its great wings flap and it rises to thirty thousand miles in the sky, then flies south for three months before landing.[125]

The P'eng is so large that just taking flight requires an enormous effort, and it only succeeds if a typhoon wind helps to lift it up. And yet when a tiny cicada and a fledgling dove hear about the P'eng they laugh derisively. "When we want to fly," they say, "we can easily reach the lower branches of small trees."[126]

Compared to the cicada and the dove, the P'eng is so enormous we might assume that with one flap of its mighty wings it could instantly leave both of them behind. But because the P'eng is so much larger, it must also travel a vast distance before it can land. The leap that appears like an instant to the P'eng seems like three boring months to the cicada and dove.

Chuang Tzu's point is that "large" and "small" or "long" and "short" aren't contradictory at all but relative and relational. Each of them depends on our point of view. Everything is large and small at the same time—large and small to differing degrees. What holds true for these properties holds true as well for every condition of being: old and young, wise and rash, good and bad. You can't have anything without its opposite. Each creates and sustains the other. Chuang Tzu takes us, in other words, from contradiction to complexity. And he takes us from a revolutionary view of time to something very different.

Among the things that Chuang Tzu wanted to resist was the Confucian mental architecture that Seijo and her husband were trying to escape. The Confucians saw complexity as dangerous because it threatened to overturn the order they taught that Heaven had decreed. What Chuang Tzu called "complexity" they called "contradiction," just as Western thinkers might. But Chuang Tzu said that contradictions aren't real. They only seem to pose a problem when we assume that something can exist in isolation.

The Confucians said we need to think objectively. If multiple witnesses to an event give us accounts that don't correspond, we should try to weed the variations out until we reach a level of basic fact. But Chuang Tzu hoped to find another way. Instead of looking for a single point of view, he wanted to embrace all of them as real. For him it seemed impossible not to see things differently from differing perspectives, and he thought that leaving the perspectives out would mean losing the most important information. You couldn't understand what made the P'eng's world unique by looking through the eyes of the cicada or dove.

But once we stop searching for a single truth, how are we supposed to make any sense of things? For Chuang Tzu the key to this dilemma is time. Our differing perceptions don't have to agree. In the early morning mist a tree might look blue. At noon it could be a brilliant green. As the sun sets it might turn deep brown. Instead of selecting only one account as true, we can see each of them as moments in time that create a sequence or a kind of flow.[127] The closest analogy in the modern world might be the notes in a musical score. Choosing only one moment as the truth would be as absurd as trying to hear just one note of an entire symphony. Chuang Tzu was intrigued by what the music would do next. When it paused, he'd pause, and when the tempo picked up, he was prepared to match the pace. The point of listening was not to reach the end, but to enjoy the beauty of complexity itself. Fast or slow—who would want the music to stop?

What makes the whole performance most exciting, Chuang Tzu said, is that we ourselves are a part of it. But what about poor Seijo—caught between two worlds? From his perspective Chuang Tzu might say to her, "What did you expect? Life itself is a play of opposites. When you're at home, you want to be away. When you're away, you'll want to be at home. And when you get back, naturally it's not the same. One moment we're fish living in the sea, then we're giant birds flying through the air— it's all quite unnerving until we understand that none of us make these moves by ourselves. It's a symphony, not a solo gig. Try to enjoy being part of it all."

Seijo's story ends when the two become one. But according to Chuang Tzu they've always been that way. He'd also say we'll never get to see that "one" if we keep our eyes fixed on Seijo alone. To find the "one" we have to think symphonically. We have take in the whole performance: the parents, the husband, and the house and the town, the two kids and Seijo too. The cast of characters will change again and again, but the oneness of it all will go on forever.

TIME-BEING AND BEING-TIME

Chuang Tzu didn't ask if the world would ever end. The question seems never to have come to mind. But he might have said with some degree of confidence that every future moment is bound to be just as complex as the one we're in right now. The present moment isn't a darkened mirror, and in the future there won't be a "face to face." Instead, the sun will rise, the night will fall. Winter will bring snow, the rains will come in spring. In a changing world, change itself is the way.

Yet there's still something about time that Chuang Tzu doesn't see, something his crazy stories overlook. He missed what Dogen Zenji has in mind in his writings on *uji* or "time-being":

> An ancient buddha said:
> For the time being stand on top of the highest peak.
> For the time being proceed along the bottom of the deepest
>   ocean.
> For the time being three heads and eight arms.
> For the time being an eight- or sixteen-foot body.
> For the time being a staff or whisk.
> For the time being a pillar or lantern.
> For the time being the sons of Zhang or Li.
> For the time being the earth and sky.[128]

Time—the ancient Buddha—can be understood as the unfolding of ceaseless change. One moment it places us amid the mountain peaks, the next at the "bottom of the deepest ocean." One moment, time shows us a staff or whisk. Next, a pillar or a lantern comes into view. Dogen says that this dimension of time is real, the dimension of ceaseless change or flow. But he wants us to look at time with greater care so we'll understand its real complexity.

Ordinarily we conceive of time as a succession of discrete events. As each moment comes and goes, we leave it behind. But actually time is not the same as space. You can never be in two places at once, but Dogen claims that you can be in two different times. The time that flows is one dimension, to be sure, but there's a second dimension as well.

One morning you're racing to get off to work. All you can think about is what you have to do. You jump into the shower, step out, and brush your teeth. Throwing on your clothes, you run downstairs. You grab a cup of coffee and read through your notes. With your clipboard in hand you walk out to the car. But then, as you get in, the phone starts to buzz. The meeting's been called off—and you can come in late. Suddenly you don't know what to do. The kids are at school. Your wife has left. You get out, stand up, and walk behind the house, where you sit on a bench staring at the trees. Suddenly you feel the pull of time let go and everything around you seems alive and bright, absolutely calm and motionless. It's as though you're on an island while the river flows by.

This is what Dogen saw that Chuang Tzu overlooked. This is what remained when Nansen's cat was cut in two, and what the Buddha found at his awakening. Time flows like a river or a symphony. But it's true as well that certain moments of our lives have a timeless or eternal character. And then, the here and now becomes everything. The mind has stopped trying to go anywhere, and the boundary between the self and world dissolves.

When Seijo comes back to her ancestral home, her life is like a pile of old photographs she can't seem to arrange in the proper way. Long ago she was a good daughter who dreamed of her happy future with the man she loved. Then she was the rebel fleeing in the night, and then a revolutionary in the hills. Now she finds herself back in the suburbs again, with parents who are worried what the neighbors will say. These moments look so discontinuous that no arrangement, it would seem, can make them cohere into something like a unity.

And yet, as the koan tells us, somehow they do. When Seijo leaves the boat and goes up to her room, the two Seijos suddenly meld into one. To anyone who hears the story for the first time, that moment must sound astonishing. It seems magical and miraculous. But maybe it's not a miracle at all. Maybe it's something that takes place every day—in fact, at every moment of our lives. No matter how divided our minds might be, no matter how circuitous the route we take, it all comes together in the here and now. What happens to Seijo happens to each of us.

Every moment, Dogen says, is actually eternal, unified, and perfect even though we notice this wholeness only once in a while, as Seijo does when she fuses with herself. But as he points out, every moment also flows. Both are dimensions of the real, both are dimensions of time. So then he asks a question that might never occur to anyone who hasn't spent thirty years sitting on a cushion watching time oscillate between change and motionless eternity.

Remember Goso's "Are they one or are they two?" Well, Dogen knew exactly what Goso meant. How can the two dimensions co-exist—the one that flows and the one forever motionless? What could ever join them in a unified way? Perhaps surprisingly, Dogen's answer is "You."

The oneness of the moment happens automatically, without any effort or reflection on our part. The unconscious Buddha mind does its work without our even noticing. But ordinary consciousness shouldn't be dismissed as deluding or unworthy of respect. It also has a crucial job to do—it's the one that puts the flow into flowing time, and without it "nothing would flow," as Dogen says.[129] Ordinary consciousness and Buddha mind aren't opposed but complementary. The same is true for flowing time and the eternal.

Our real problem isn't that we're clueless and caught between right and left, up and down. The real problem is that we don't appreciate how much we accomplish every day, just by bathing children or making beds, writing legal briefs or nailing shingles to a roof. The briefs, the beds, the shingles aren't what's important. These objects in themselves are mere eternities, stranded like whales beached on the shore. But we ourselves are the ones that bring them to life. The most important work we humans do is to create the "flow" that weaves eternities together in a way that makes a timeless universe into a home for temporal beings.

EXILE OR AN ECOLOGY OF MIND?

Revolutionary thinking in the West has tried to solve in a different way the problem of contradiction in our lives. The Apostle Paul's revolution was just the start. Every revolution since the fall of Rome has been a dress rehearsal for the end of time, when the biggest contradiction of them all will end—between good and evil, heaven and hell. Until then, exile will be our fate. We're supposed to live as strangers in a strange land, or pilgrims on a pilgrimage—"not of this world," just as the Bible says.[130]

On the eve of World War II, the literary critic Walter Benjamin wrote an influential essay where he evoked a figure called "the Angel of History."[131] As the Angel watches the horizon of time, a wind blowing fiercely from behind him sweeps along the ruins of the past like so much trash. You can see the wreckage rushing by in the wind—the pieces of crockery, baby shoes, broken furniture, ropes and rusting knives, all left behind by our violent past. Before the Angel's eyes these ruins start to collect, and as he walks backward, the pile grows until it vaults into the sky. Benjamin tells us that the Angel never sees anything except these fragments of calamity, but all the while, despite of the mounting evidence of ruin, the Angel is backing into paradise.

This story expresses a painful truth. Whatever good people have managed to do, they've had to do it against enormous odds, often unaware of how their suffering would benefit those who came after them. Revolutionary hope is the belief that if we just keep trying, things will improve even though they often seem to be getting worse. For those alive today there's no chance of paradise, but if we're still willing to push ahead, we can help to make it a reality for some generation coming after us.

But the cost of paradise is the Everest of ruins. Marxists like Benjamin would agree with the most pro-market of entrepreneurs: creative destruction is the road we have to take. We don't have the luxury of turning back.

Dogen understood, quite as much as Benjamin, that life involves a great deal of suffering and loss. No one except a Buddha always feels completely at one with the moment. But retreating from that moment is not the way of Zen. The way is to accept everything that arrives without the expectation of anything else. And when we do, the whole terrain will be transformed. The wasteland becomes the paradise we're looking for. Awakened mind has this basic openness. In the Lotus Sutra it's compared to falling rain:

> The rain falls everywhere,
> Coming from all sides,
> Flowing everywhere without limit,
> Reaching over the face of the earth.
>
> Into the hidden recesses of the mountains, streams, and steep
>   valleys
> Where plants and trees grow, and medicinal herbs,
> Big trees and small,

A hundred [varieties of grain], rice seedling, sugar cane, and
   grapevines

All are moistened by the rain,
And abundantly enriched.
The dry ground is soaked,
And both herbs and trees flourish....

Plants, trees, thickets, and forest,
According to their need, receive moisture...
Roots, stems, branches, and leaves
Blossoms and fruit in brilliant color.[132]

There's nothing that the rain will ever refuse; there's no place it cannot flow.
No matter what it meets, it will always bestow itself to nourish all beings.

Earlier, I wrote that revolution is more than a fact of history. It's also a
frame of mind that looks to the future for deliverance from our problems
today. But the Buddhist view of time also creates its own distinctive frame
of mind, the one suggested by the Lotus Sutra itself. As each new item on
the list appears—the trees big and small, the valleys and streams—the addi-
tion just creates a greater unity. We could go on adding items day after day
without destroying the coherence already there.

The logic of Buddhism is inclusiveness. The point is never to reject, and
certainly never to destroy, but to find a way of fitting everything in. As the
great master Pai Chang taught, we shouldn't even seek to rid ourselves of
our flaws, problems, and serious mistakes. He said that the sages of ancient
times looked on suffering and sickness "as medicines." "Troubles and diffi-
culties" they embraced as though they were "freedom and ease." "Obstacles and barriers" became "liberation" and "delusions" were "companions to
Reality."[133]

Of course, this task is sometimes quite challenging, and it doesn't always
go as well as we'd like. But the model of change that all of this implies is
evolutionary, not revolutionary. It offers an image of the world as a living
system whose coherence remains undiminished in the midst of constant

growth and decay. It would be a mistake to suppose that when Chuang Tzu, Dogen, and the Lotus Sutra draw on nature to describe reality, their mountains, streams, giant fish, and doves are simply ornaments to enliven what they say. When they conceive of a life lived with skill, they imagine something like an ecology—an ecology whose focus is the relationship between the mind and a complex world. They teach what we might call an "ecology of mind."

This term was coined about fifty years ago by an anthropologist, Gregory Bateson. At the time Bateson started to believe that the West had fundamentally misunderstood what consciousness was all about. Drawing on fields still new in the seventies—cybernetics, information theory, and the beginning science of complexity—Bateson saw a striking similarity between the operations of the mind and those of complex systems in the natural world. Traditional thinking about the mind had involved reason and the truth or falsity of propositions. But Bateson pushed those concerns to the side. He argued that ideas weren't real at all and couldn't ever be. Ideas were only images. What mattered were the actual ways of life that these images made possible. Did they create harmony and understanding or did they create suspicion? Did they create compassion or violence?

Bateson's arguments wouldn't have surprised thinkers in East Asia, but they were so new and unfamiliar in the West that many people failed to appreciate their remarkable implications. Not only did his writings undermine the hope that our ideas can ever be real, they also called into doubt the belief that we can solve our problems by changing the world without also changing ourselves. Mind and world are inseparable. It's impossible to know where one begins and the other stops.

But to say that mind and world are somehow one is to question a most basic Western paradigm. When we think this way we've started to erase the line between humans and the rest of Creation. So long as we continue to preserve that line, we can see the destiny of the human race as separate from the fate of the universe. Indeed, that's the job of the Apocalypse—to lift humanity out of nature's time, vast and cyclical as it seems to be.

But what if we restore humanity to the whole that is nature's time?

CHAPTER 6:
IMAGES OF ORDER
IN A COMPLEX WORLD

K oans can be deceptively simple. Here, for example, is another famous case:

> A monk asked Master Chimon, "What will the lotus flower be before it has come out of the water?" Chimon said, "The lotus flower."[134]

Because it's a koan we already know it's making some point about enlightenment. And like many koans, this one sets some sort of trap. There must a subtle inconsistency nudging us to see things in a different way. But the question seems so innocuous it's hard to know where we should begin.

The lotus itself is a crucial clue.

From ancient times in the Eastern world, the lotus flower has symbolized the natural process of change and growth. Lotus bulbs are planted in a pond or lake, and gradually they sprout, rising from the muck. Murky at the bottom, the water becomes more clear and bright as the lotus shoot makes its way to the top, gradually transforming into a bud. Finally the bud will leave the water behind, raising itself into the air where it waits until it opens to the sun.

The perfection of the lotus is a special kind—a perfection that develops gradually. And so the lotus is a symbol, we could say, of the way our own lives might unfold over time. Each stage in the growth of the lotus brings about something like a purification. The lotus travels from the darkness into the light, from the coarsest element of earth into the most refined of elements, air. Born in filth, it becomes spotlessly clean. And out of chaos it manages to produce an exquisite symmetry. Who among us wouldn't want to do the same?

The lotus is beautiful in its own right, but that's not the only reason it's so widely used in gardens from India to Japan, and from Sri Lanka to Nepal. A symbol of perfection, wholeness, unity, the lotus is the consummate flower for gardens that are meant to be an image of order. From these gardens we can learn how to live—how to overcome our own obstacles and achieve something better.

The monk's question, then, is quite a loaded one. It's concerned with lotuses and gardens, that's true, but also with the state of mind the flower signifies. If Zen is indeed an "ecology of mind," then what kind of order does it reveal? What kind of harmony will we find if we practice long and hard enough?

Before the lotus flower opens to display the perfection of its final form, it has to struggle blindly in the darkness underneath. Perhaps that's the way the monk sees himself. He wants to reach the goal but he doesn't know how. To him, his life looks so imperfect and confused that the lotus seems all the more beautiful. If only he could reach a perfection like that! Most of us probably feel the same way.

ZEN GARDENS AND ZEN PSYCHOLOGY

Zen and gardens share a long history. Gardening and viewing gardens both belong to a larger family of Zen arts that include calligraphy, the way of tea, and *ikebana*, the arrangement of flowers. Even though they have the formal elements we associate with art in the West, what matters most in Zen might be described as the psychology. After all, Zen teaches that world and mind aren't separate as they appear to be, but fundamentally unified. Words and ideas cut the world in two. Consciousness itself creates an "I" and "me" that makes the world into an "it" or "you." But Zen has devised an array of arts that help us recover the basic unity.

Of course these aren't the only activities that can produce a changed state of mind. When we wash the dishes too, there's more at stake than a little grease. As we tidy up the room or even comb our hair, we're structuring our consciousness in a different way. To some degree everybody understands that the order we create outside ourselves becomes an order inside too. But in Zen, "inside" and "outside" don't exist. The point is to dissolve that boundary. And this makes the Zen arts somewhat unique.

Among the many arts that Zen has devised, gardening occupies a special place because the garden is an image of the universe when it is viewed through awakened eyes. It embodies in a material form the opposing principles that make the world whole: unity and differentiation, artfulness and play, careful cultivation and wildness. To these we could add other elements as well—permanence and change, closure and openness, austere restraint and sensuality. The order that the Zen garden represents emerges from this balance of opposites, the same balance that we should try to maintain in our practice and our lives.

In a garden tended the proper way, the forces that create instability can become protectors of a universal order. You can see this lesson almost everywhere you turn. There might be a Japanese maple whose trunk has grown out of balance, tilting to the left. Seeing this, a good gardener will take care to train the tree in a way that creates a countervailing motion. If the trunk is leaning to the left, then at least one major branch should grow to the right, while some branches on the left are cut away. Out of this asymmetry a balance comes, a balance that somehow seems more alive than the balance offered by mere symmetry.

Symmetry, so favored by the West, creates a balance that appears to express a timeless, unchanging state of things. But in reality nothing stays the same, and so the balance that arises from symmetry might be seen as going against the Tao, the flow. The asymmetry of Asian gardening is meant to emphasize the element of time. It creates a sense of natural motion that unfolds like a music for the eye. When we see the maple, it doesn't move, and yet its form expresses a contrapuntal motion. Implicitly it tells us that we shouldn't be afraid. Out of the randomness of change, a deeper, self-organizing harmony will gradually manifest itself. We can live more skillfully if we try not to resist change but to look for an emerging order as we go along. Change, not stasis, is the way.

Asymmetrical balance and motionless motion are principles that shape the garden as a whole. And openness and closure are two crucial elements that help produce these overarching effects. A pond, for example, creates an open space. The pond brings the sky down to the earth, and indeed, on a clear, windless day you can see reflections of the passing clouds. At night you can see a second moon, shimmering right there below your feet. Yet if you stare too long, you might begin to feel that you've gotten lost in the groundlessness. Which way is up and which way is down? Which is the reflection and which is the real? And so we need to balance the openness with, say, a corresponding mass of trees, to make an enclosure that shelters and protects. Once we feel safe, we'll be more relaxed. We want some openness, but not too much. The greater the openness created by the pond, the heavier the corresponding mass needs to be.

This balance of openness and closure should repeat everywhere you turn to look. The garden as a whole should have a rhythm of its own, a counterpoint that makes it seem alive in a way we might not notice consciously but that still teaches us how we should respond to events as they naturally arise.

Because of its openness to the sky, the garden pond defines a special space, and in no other place can the lotus grow. It rises up from the muck into the sun, and when it flowers, the yellow, white, or pink creates another kind of counterpoint against the water's dark, amorphous mass of green. In some of the gardens you can see, the lotuses will cover the pond's whole expanse. There's something truly astonishing about a quarter acre of lotuses, all of them appearing to flower at once. Seeing such a scene, many of us might think, "This is how our lives could be."

In Tibetan Buddhism there's a famous prayer. "*Om mani padme hung*," the Tibetans recite—"Hail, the jewel in the lotus." The "jewel in the lotus" to which they refer is the enlightened mind in the midst of things. The lotus is the jewel of the garden, we might say. And our minds can become like the lotus too, calm and perfect at the center of it all. When this happens, everything will be revealed as a garden of enlightenment.

If we take the lesson of the lotus as our guide, it's possible to think about Zen as leading us toward a certain kind of life—beautiful, orderly, and unified. Perhaps this is what the monk wanted to achieve. On and off the cushion, we are gardening. When you get home you might look at your room and realize it's cluttered and disorderly. If it doesn't give your mind the right sense of peace, you could rearrange your furniture to imbue the space with a better mood. Or you might create more balance in your routine. If you get up early to do zazen, you can take that stillness with you through a day that's probably filled with all sorts of craziness. Even if you don't practice meditation, you can open spaces in your routine—going out to lunch instead of eating at your desk, pausing to drink a quiet cup of tea before the kids return from school. You can be the gardener of your life.

For centuries Zen teachers have tried to employ the elements of gardening to convey lessons about enlightenment. In a wordless and unthinking way, much can be learned from the enjoyment of these gardens, which is a kind of meditation in itself. And yet, even though all of this might be true, the matter—as always—is really more complex.

WHEN THINGS FALL APART—NATURALLY

Buddhists aren't the only ones to revere some image of a perfect harmony. Eden, remember, was a garden too. In different ways, perhaps, all of us would like to see an ultimate perfection finally revealed, laid out with mandala-like clarity. Not just religion but the arts and sciences—aren't they also motivated by this dream? Doesn't our knowledge always aspire to getting the whole picture right finally? When we say of a thinker that he's written the last word, we've paid him the very highest complement. Perhaps the last word is a dream we all share—physicists and poets, chemists and engineers, surgeons, marketers, and diplomats.

And yet no matter how close we might come, the fulfillment of that dream seems to slip away. Just as we're moving the last piece into place, suddenly everything falls apart again. And when it does, the results can be catastrophic.

Both perfection and catastrophe were the subjects of an essay Paul Krugman wrote for the *New York Times* a little more than a year after the financial collapse of 2008.[135] He asked how his fellow economists had failed to predict the disaster that took place. Indeed, just before the stock market plunged, most of his colleagues were totally convinced that their field had spoken the last word on financial stability.

In the past, economics was a battlefield of fiercely contesting opinions, but not long ago the whole discipline achieved what one eminent authority described as a "broad convergence of vision." Only four years prior to the collapse, a leading figure had addressed their national convention. To loud applause he boldly declared that they had solved the problem of recurrent depressions.

But then, as Krugman noted, it all came undone. The predictive failure was bad enough, he wrote, but even more destructive was the overconfidence. Economists believed they simply knew too much. Their knowledge was so perfect it just couldn't fail.

In the koan above, the monk asks Chimon what the lotus flower will be before it rises into the air and light. But Chimon doesn't give the answer we'd expect. He doesn't say that it will be a lotus bud. Instead he says again that it will be the lotus flower. Perhaps by answering as he did, Chimon meant to help his student recognize a basic problem with the way the question was framed. Something about perfection has been overlooked, something the monk might have pushed aside.

When Krugman himself tried to explain how economists had gotten things so wrong, he made a pitch for his own approach, which favors intervention by the government over unrestricted markets. But for all his brilliance, he seemed to overlook a problem even bigger than an overreliance on a single point of view. Every approach, even Krugman's own, achieves its formal consistency by excluding whatever doesn't fit. Like the perfection of the Japanese garden, the perfection glimpsed by economists was in fact illusory.

Nowadays many cities in the U.S. have Asian gardens where people can go if they want to get a little taste of a Zen. In Seattle where I trained, members of our sangha would meet every week at the Asian garden for a tea ceremony. We'd sit for hours in the tea house by the pond, and often on the way out we would stop to admire the perfection of the garden all around—the pond with its lotuses, the overhanging trees, the motionless rhythm of enclosure and space.

Sometimes on the weekends the crowds would grow so large it was hard to maintain the proper mood. But, of course, the crowds were simply seeking what we'd found. Even visitors who were oblivious to the principles of Asian gardening could be deeply moved by the order they surveyed. The aesthetics came from half a world away but the garden seemed to speak to everyone.

The garden was at its very best on weekends, when the biggest crowds could be expected to arrive. But as I learned by stopping there on other days, an entire team of gardeners worked all week just to prepare. If you go on Saturday to the garden in Seattle, it seems to have existed for eternity in its present, timeless form. That's the message a good garden should convey. But if you visit on a Wednesday afternoon, you might see the workers cutting grass with their machines. Dead and dying plants have to be replaced, and plastic pots with fresh plants from the nursery will be brought in by small pickup trucks.

And what about that ancient tree which appears to have been shaped by centuries of wind and snow? If you look carefully you might see the stiff brown wire, skillfully concealed, that a gardener used to bend some essential limb. It's quite instructive also to watch an arborist trim away unwanted branches. If the job is accomplished properly, with cuts made very close to the trunk, no marks remain when the next season comes. Like all artifice, when it's done with greatest skill, it seems to be the work of nature's hand.

And then there are unwanted plants. In the middle of the irises lining the pond, which seems to exist outside of time, loosestrife or phragmites might have taken root, perhaps from seeds dropped by some migrating bird. These invasive plants have to be pulled up by hand, but in the grass and under the canopy, gardeners use weed-whackers powered by gas, cutting through the garden's serenity with a ripping, buzzing noise. Once I even watched them spraying herbicides, toxic chemicals that leach into the streams where they collect in the tissues of fish swimming in the Puget Sound. Needless to say, they use other chemicals—fertilizers to make the grass bright green, and algaecides to clear the water in the lotus pond.

If the workers were to let the garden go, it wouldn't look at all the way it does. Neglected, the exotics would soon die away—the beautiful trees and bushes from Japan. Unwanted species would rapidly invade. Clinging vines would smother the low-growing maples, which only live about a century at best. Over time, debris would gather in the pond, and gradually the open water would become a swamp. Chokeberry, milkweed, and thistles would take root, followed by sumac and locust trees.

If you returned in a hundred years, you might not give the spot a second look. The garden would have devolved into a place without any obvious coherence at all, no beauty, balance, or harmony—an unattractive jumble of this and that, what you can see by the road every day. And yet, which is really more natural: the well-tended garden or the abandoned patch?

IMAGES OF ORDER VERSUS ORDER ITSELF

The garden seems so perfect we can make the same mistake as Krugman's economists. In such cases what we see are *images*—images of order we ourselves have made. But nature's real order is something else again. Maybe that's what Chimon was hinting to the monk.

We create our images of order by excluding all the things we can't fit in, things that work against our expectations even though they're part of our world somehow. And then we mistake these images for the way things really are.

In Zen we sometimes speak about the finger and the moon. The finger pointing at the moon is supposed to steer our eyes to the moon itself. And sometimes, pointing with a finger helps. But the relationship can get reversed. We start to treat the symbol as though it were real. Of course we do this all the time.

The natural world lacks the balanced harmonies that define the classical Japanese garden. And even if we hike into a forest or a park, we tend to look for places that will agree with our expectations about the kind of scene we should admire as "beautiful." But on our way to special places of this kind—on our way to images of order—we overlook countless other views that seem unimportant or disorderly. Now we've mistaken the finger for the moon: distracted by the mental image, we ignore the real.

What holds true for gardens and forest hikes holds true as well for intellectual life, even though we make a special effort to deny that any such confusion is at work. We want to believe that our total stock of knowledge keeps growing larger and more perfect day by day. At the same time, the sum of what we don't know seems to be shrinking proportionally.

In reality, this may not be the case. Even though we know much more than people did only a hundred years ago, the sum of our ignorance has also increased. We have more uncertainties than they ever did, more questions and new areas to explore. Indeed, what counts as "knowledge" never ceases to change. Nobody studies Natural Philosophy today. Scientists no longer look for a cosmic ether or investigate animal magnetism. "Facts" that seemed obvious not so long ago turn out to depend on beliefs we now dismiss as untrue and absurd. The work of every generation seems to overturn much that its predecessors struggled to achieve. And yet we don't stop to think about the implications. What we call knowledge might actually be another example of the images of order we've mistaken for the real.

Until the recession of 2008, the biggest failure of our economy had taken place in 1929, a global collapse that left unemployed about a quarter of all Americans. The stock market fell almost as far as it could go, and billions of dollars went up in smoke. When we remember catastrophes like that, we want to believe that people at the time knew much less than we do today.

But back in 1928 they really knew quite a lot. There were many brilliant economists who wrote enormous and sophisticated books filled with elaborate theories. If you live near a good library, many of these books are still sitting on the shelves, unread and gathering a century of dust. But at the time, their knowledge seemed to work. It seemed to show that ignorance was in retreat. And as for economic instability, it appeared to be a thing of the distant past, a problem that science had resolved. Then one day this knowledge shattered like glass, and with it the whole world of finance.

Around that same time many people believed that a solution had been found for another problem as well. Almost every educated person in the West was convinced that war had been overcome by the steady forward march of history.[136] There were many books with titles like *The End of War*, and most of the world's leaders were quite confident that modern diplomacy and smarter legislation had created systems that couldn't fail. Experts could be counted on to know what to do. Unlike the amateurs of ages past, they had the skills and the knowledge to avoid any sort of large-scale catastrophe.

But then in 1914 war broke out. In fact, it was the biggest war the world had ever seen. All the sophisticated systems designed to keep conflict from happening were quickly retooled to make the war itself more efficient and well-organized. The death toll was the highest in history. And only a few decades after that, a second conflict—World War II—began. At the time, the Germans were thought to be the best educated nation anywhere. In many fields of knowledge they were preeminent. Who would have predicted Hitler's rise, or the nightmare of the Holocaust? The modern era was supposed to leave behind this sort of barbarity.

Two world wars, perhaps a hundred million dead. So much for modern political science and the profession of diplomacy. So much for the value of mass education. I don't mean to suggest that these are fraudulent, or that they shouldn't be pursued. But there's something here that we haven't understood. When it comes to the structures we create, are we looking at the finger or the moon? Do we see the lotus for what it really is, or are we only seeing what we want to see?

If you look at economic history, you'll notice that collapses go all the way back to the beginning of civilization. And sadly, the same is true for war. But every time things fall apart again, people seem absolutely amazed. How could this happen? we ask with disbelief. Maybe it really is the end of the world. Maybe the Apocalypse is on the way. But our fantasies of the Apocalypse are just the other side of the same coin—the other side of our images of order. We want to believe we're getting closer to the truth, to a perfect knowledge that leaves nothing out. But what if knowledge can't be perfected in this way?

There's something noble about the desire that motivates those who search for truth, people like Krugman's economists. They look at the market's fluctuations and they say, "How can we prevent the catastrophic collapse that has caused so much suffering?" To answer this question they lose a lot of sleep. They toss and turn on their beds at night. They put in eighty hours every week trying to unearth the secrets that will make the system work impeccably.

But economists aren't the only ones whose search for order causes them to lose sleep. Over in the English Department it's the same. There, instead of the market's fluctuations, the subject is fiction or poetry. "How can I talk about this novel?" they ask, "How can I explain what the author really meant?" When literary critics do this sort of thing, they struggle with confusion that appears to have no end. You try this approach and it doesn't seem to work. You try something else and it fails again. But after all the missteps and dead ends, you find something that seems to work a little bit. And that's like a cup of cool water in a drought. Refreshed, you trudge on until you find another piece that somehow adds to the overall coherence. Gradually, the pieces assemble to fill in what remains of the puzzle. All this can take a whole life or many lives, since younger people might pick up where you left off.

Scientists know this routine quite well. Only a small percentage of experiments turn out to have the predicted results. Scientists encounter failure most of the time. And even their successes are often transient. Past findings get overturned by fresh research. New technologies can make obsolete the methods used for many years. Yet, despite the setbacks and failures they face, the dream of order keeps the sciences going. Every once in a while research will cohere in a truly spectacular way, and then someone wins the Nobel Prize. But the grants and the prizes aren't really the goal—the goal is the beauty of the order itself.

Searching for such order is a part of human life. And yet, we might not understand what we've done when we've encountered it. Have we revealed the way things are, or have we simply made an image of a world that's really too complex for any image to reflect in a flawless way? That would explain why our knowledge falls apart.

Just before the recession of 2008, America's economists had gathered to hear the leading figures celebrate the garden they'd made. For just a moment, the lotus opened up and a real perfection seemed to be achieved. All of us look forward to such moments now and then, and, if we're lucky, one comes our way. When that happens, we might wish that it could last forever. And naturally we'd like to see it happen again. Then, when it doesn't, we often blame ourselves. If only we had somehow done things differently, maybe then we'd see another blossoming.

This is the way that Krugman seems to think. He says that his colleagues went off the rails simply because of an omission. Relying too much on the pro-market view, they overlooked the need for government control. More regulations, instead of less, would have prevented the collapse. But actually this might not be altogether true. Maybe the collapse might have been forestalled, but more regulations would have brought with them a different set of problems—problems like slow growth and higher joblessness. Eventually, both systems would fail in different ways, the one with regulations and the one with less. Too much control will produce stagnation, but too little breeds the recklessness that nearly destroyed the world economy. We want to believe that we can finally get it right, and that one last crucial piece of evidence will solve the mystery once and for all. But no matter how carefully we plan, no matter how we tend our gardens of the mind, some detail will always get left out. And that's just the one that will catch us by surprise.

NO "WORLD," MIND ONLY

Why does our knowledge keep falling apart? Why does it seem that the dream of perfect order always lies beyond our reach? In the latter part of the Ming Dynasty, the Chinese master Te-Ch'ing wrote these words:

> Intrinsically, there is no body, mind, or world, nor are there any deluded thoughts and emotional conceptions. Right at this moment…everything that manifests before you [is] illusory and insubstantial—all…are reflections projected from the…mind.[137]

The claim that everything is unreal often gets repeated in the Mahayana teachings, and so does the idea that everything we see is just a projection of the mind. Yet of all claims the Mahayana makes, these are the hardest to take seriously. How can anybody actually believe that the table I'm writing on isn't real, or the tree I see outside my window now, or the car I drove to work an hour ago? Surely these aren't illusory.

But Te-Ch'ing doesn't mean what we might think. If you run at full force into a brick wall, you'll quite predictably knock yourself cold. If you don't drink water for four or five days, your kidneys will fail and your heart will stop—that's an absolute certainty. Buddhism has no trouble with these facts, and any tradition that rejected them should have vanished long ago from the earth. Te-Ch'ing means that our idea of the "real" is just an image of what actually exists, an imperfect image of perfection made from the bits and pieces of our experience.[138] "Body," "world," and even "mind" are simply fabrications. The conscious mind can only perceive as real what the structures it has made allow it to, and so the world as it really is might not exist in the form that we suppose.

The point of Zen isn't to lift the veil, revealing a perfect image of everything. Behind every veil there will be another one—yet another image that our conscious minds make up to deal with the complexity. Veil will follow veil ad infinitum, and no resolution can ever be reached, not even if the universe itself should end. Instead, the point of Zen is to help us understand where all our images are coming from. This is the heart of Zen's ecology of mind. And Te-Ch'ing says that they have just one source: the unconscious Buddha mind, which he describes as "vast and open, bright and luminous—intrinsically perfect and complete." To see this mind directly is enlightenment.

In other words, an enlightened human being starts out like a person in a dark theater caught up with the action on the screen. But for some reason, maybe boredom or disgust, she stops watching and turns around in her seat. To her utter astonishment, she discovers that the images on the screen aren't real but only projections. And they're coming from a source behind the wall! Te-Ch'ing says that when this occurs, the viewer's awareness will never be the same. Looking straight at the projector she can understand that the whole movie's nothing but the play of light.[139]

Let's say that this account is accurate. Let's say the mind really is like a projector and that the images we see on the screen have never been real as we believed. So, what happens after that? What do enlightened people see once they've awakened?

In another place—this time, a poem—Te-Ch'ing gives an answer to that:

> The ten thousand things
> Arise and disappear
> Without any reason.[140]

"The ten thousand things" in Chinese poetry is a stock phrase signifying "everything"—everything in the whole universe. Te-Ch'ing means that enlightened human beings go back to watching the movie. But now they watch it in a different way. Even after the breakthrough of enlightenment, all that the conscious mind can ever know are the images of reality and not reality "in itself," whatever that might actually mean. But knowing that they're only images can be liberating. Things no longer have a "reason" in the sense that we now regard them as a kind of play. As they unfold we're no longer required to look on them with dread and awe.

No one who goes to a movie believes that they should scream "Watch out!" when the hero is in danger. When there's a tragic death we might shed some tears. Maybe we soak a few handkerchiefs. Yet no one really thinks that the actress has died. People might be troubled by the message of a movie, but it would be insane to treat fictional events as though they've actually occurred. The pleasure of going to a movie comes from the playful way it lets us experience the moment. And this playfulness can make us more animated than our own lives sometimes do.

One reason for the pleasure movies give is that they take away the danger. The hero could be in great danger, certainly. The plot might involve leaping to a moving train from a hovering helicopter, or running from an ammo dump before it explodes into shrapnel and flames. Movies can show such extraordinary peril because they never endanger us. They allow us to savor the adventure of life without having to undergo the risks.

This doesn't mean we don't identify with the characters on the screen. We laugh when they laugh, we cry when they cry, but there's always a sense of safety or well-being while we're reclining in our seats. If this sense of safety were to disappear, few of us would go to watch the movies anymore. We'd stop watching movies, or we'd try, if we somehow lost the ability to distance ourselves from the action on the screen. Then we'd really cry when the daughter dies. We'd really shriek with terror or recoil with pain when the slasher wields his bloodied knife. Under those circumstances, movies would become as fear-inducing as the world that we call "real".

We might assume that seeing the real world as a play would make us indifferent to the suffering of others—and this would be true if conscious-ness were indeed the limits of awareness. But when the conscious mind has been set free from the paralyzing force of awe and fear, compassion rises up from a deeper place—astonishing, boundless, indiscriminate. And then a deeper intelligence can tell us what to do. It's as though we step into the movie itself, acting to help others with serene confidence.

LOTUS ALL THE WAY

Seeing the projector can set us free because it helps preserve a sense of security amid great confusion and suffering. In this regard it might be help-ful to know a little bit about Te-Ch'ing's own life. At the time of his enlight-enment, Chinese Zen was in a steep decline, partly because of its rivals, the Confucians. Their plan was to cut the Buddhists off from education, fund-ing, and respectability. Toward the end of the Ming their plan had worked out well, but Te-Ch'ing was a remarkable monk, practicing with extraordi-nary diligence even though the temple system had decayed. He had his great awakening while he was still young, but he couldn't find a single teacher qualified to sanction what had happened to him. Many teachers of the time were just empty robes, spouting Zen platitudes without having gained genuine experience.

Following his enlightenment, Te-Ch'ing dedicated all his energies to reconstructing the edifice of Zen, and, despite the enormous odds, after many years, everything seemed poised to go exactly as he'd planned. His dream was to build a new monastic center that would train students from all across China. Had this plan been realized fully, Te-Ch'ing could have launched a Buddhist Renaissance. But then, as often happens, things fell apart. The intrigues of his supporters at the emperor's court brought him down along with them, even though he was innocent. His new monastery on Mt. Luoshan was burned to the ground. Te-Ch'ing was "defrocked"— forced to enter lay life. Stripped of his honors, he was left without support. And so the great dharma garden of his dreams never became a reality.[141]

Te-Ch'ing's story is remarkable precisely because he achieved so much despite the ups and downs. Eventually pardoned, he took up his vows again, and even in the period of his disgrace he wrote incessantly on Zen. A number of his writings are quite magnificent, and they often teach one lesson in particular: he reminds us that when we watch the world of form, we're watching the play of reflections in a mirror, never the real things-in-themselves.

This insight was the source of his fearlessness. It gave him an imperturbable calm and an energy that never ceased. As Te-Ch'ing clearly understood, the "three poisons" of delusion, anger, and greed have no beginning and no end, and yet the bodhisattva's vow is always to keep helping people get free from them. This might sound a bit like the myth of Sisyphus, whom the gods condemned to roll a large stone up a steep mountain for all eternity, only to have it roll back down just before it reached the summit. But what if Sisyphus could have recognized that the mountain, the stone, and everything else were a dream, a movie that he himself was making? Perhaps he might have seen it then as a great adventure, a chance to express his own creativity and to experience the life of everything as his own life too.

Another way to put it might be like this. The conscious mind won't ever completely understand, but it can't prevent itself from reaching for the perfect, final explanation. That's what the conscious mind is supposed to do. Yet even if this life can't be understood, it can be embraced in a way that restores its fundamental unity, a unity we can't know consciously but which, all the same, is completely real.

We can represent this unity in many different ways, through the arts, philosophy, history, and science. These images of order are indispensable, but life itself is quite another thing. The most profound moments of being alive often come in a way we least expect—not when the last piece falls into place but when our precious images fail. The sacred scriptures say the sun revolves around the earth, but then one day somebody with a telescope sees that it must be the other way around. Thirteen colonies in the wilderness defeat Europe's greatest military power. The world's most vibrant economy turns out to be a giant Ponzi scheme. At moments like these, when our images fail, we feel that we're dropping into empty space. Yet then, for reasons that we'll never fully understand, something always catches us. After that, new images of order will appear, which we start perfecting until they fall apart.

The moments of free-fall can be terrifying. They can keep us on the edge and gradually erode our ability to act. When they happen, they can lead to violence, and people are often at their very worst. But no matter what, such moments won't ever stop if the universe is ever-changing and complex. And so, we can live in perpetual fear, or we can learn to live on trust. To follow the way of Zen is to choose to be "one with the trusting mind."[142] Something always catches us. Something pulls it all back together again.

Developing an unconscious sensitivity to this mysterious "something"— that's the real point of the Zen arts, rather than the beauty of the bowls for tea or the color of moss on the garden stones. Another kind of intelligence takes over when we stop reaching nervously for a perfection that's always out of reach. We become aware of a responsiveness on the other side of things. Anyone who's meditated for a while knows how this responsiveness feels. It's as though you're a fish and you suddenly infer that you must be swimming in something like the sea. It's tasteless, odorless, and completely transparent, and yet somehow it responds to you. It holds you up and gives you the oxygen you need. Most of the fish don't believe it's really there, but all the same, it's ubiquitous.

Wasn't this what Master Chimon tried to say to the monk who asked him about the flower: "What will the lotus flower be before it has come out of the water?" Chimon said, "The lotus flower."

The *image* of the lotus will keep changing forever, but the real lotus— which our small minds never see—is always fully present here and now. This doesn't mean that we exist outside of change. Change is one aspect of reality too. It means that there's a wholeness change can't destroy.

The great Western poet T.S. Eliot wrote these famous lines to describe the painful failure of our dreams:

> Between the idea
> And the reality
> Between the motion
> And the act
> Falls the Shadow[143]

For Eliot, the Shadow's presence spoils everything. It means that earthly life is fallen inescapably and that nothing we can do will ever make it whole. But there is another possibility.

When our images of order fail, we can regard it as a great tragedy. Or we can see it as the triumph of life, which is always more alive than our images. Strangely, the overthrow our ideas can bring us closer to the world instead of turning us away. The "Shadow," which always intervenes in an expected manner, could be nothing other than life itself. And when we embrace it without reservations, the terrible darkness might disappear and it can become just what Te-Ch'ing says: "vast and open, bright and luminous."

CHAPTER 7:
ON AND OFF THE ROAD
OF HISTORY

If you practice Zen you might know what this like: you're in your morning meditation and you reach the point where your mind begins growing quiet and still. You enter an empty space and time disappears. It's as though you're nowhere and everywhere at once. Then, out of the silence comes the sound of the bell, signaling the end of the period. Rising quickly, you change your clothes for work. You leave the Zen center, rushing down the stairs and breathing hard as you race to catch your bus. You climb aboard and from your seat you can see a woman running for the bus just like you. Her arms keep waving as the driver pulls away even though she seems to be standing in plain sight. Beside you, two riders argue over Iraq. A Goth boy across the aisle shoots you a look.

From a timeless place you've just returned to time, and not only time but also history. History is our collective dream—fashioned by mankind over thousands of years from the raw materials that time has given us: freedom and constraint, abundance and scarcity, suffering and happiness. To enter history is to be exposed to a constant undercurrent of hope and fear. Each new moment holds the possibility of our lives becoming more complete, but each one also threatens to take away something we've desperately wanted to keep.

When we are sitting quietly in the here and now, this is not at all how things appear. The dream of history begins to seem unreal. Once we bring the timeless together with time, we recognize it all fits together even now. The presence of the moment can be so liberating because it stops the constant pressure of the hope and fear. Nothing can add, nothing can subtract.

And yet even though it sets us free, this experience creates a problem we can't overlook. We're not in the world all by ourselves but alongside seven billion other human beings. How should we inhabit the collective dream once we've recognized it as the dream it really is?

DROPPING OUT AND BREAKING RULES

This is the question that helped to make Zen an America sensation in the 1950s. Many of the people who first got involved were on the margins of the society—artists, poets, and philosophers, most of them young, bright, and promising, but somehow disenchanted with the Progress idea. They wanted to step out of history and learn how to live in the here and now. With memories of World War II still fresh in their minds, and a nuclear attack a real possibility, Zen seemed to offer them a way of waking up from a culture of destruction.

The great manifesto of that period was Jack Kerouac's novel *On the Road*. It described the travels of a group of young men who exchanged their shot at security for the thrill of aimless wandering. And even though the characters kept moving constantly, their real destination wasn't some other place: it was a way of life different from the one chosen by most Americans. The road they chose wasn't leading to the future. Instead, it was leading to an eternity present every moment:

> We went over Berthold Pass, down to the great plateau, Tabernash, Troublesome, Kremmling; down Rabbit Ears Pass to Steamboat Springs, and out; fifty miles of dusty detour; then Craig and the Great American Desert. As we crossed the Colorado-Utah border I saw God in the sky in the form of huge gold sunburning clouds above the desert that seemed to point a finger at me and say, "Pass here and go on, you're on the road to heaven."[144]

No one expected such a revelation in the heart of America—a country whose forward motion always meant that the truth would be revealed at a later date. And yet the novel seemed to say we didn't have to wait until the

Second Coming. We could find our paradise anywhere right now, even on the Interstate. For thousands of readers this was thrilling news.

But *On the Road* gave its readers something more than such glimpses of an eternal here and now. It gave them a model for a "Zen" way of life based on a rejection of the status quo. Zen was about saying no to history—shattering conventions and letting things go. Zen meant breaking all the rules. In the popular media, Kerouac was the ultimate outsider, a poet of the streets in a lumberjack shirt, with a cigarette hanging from his pouting lips. The nation looked on with rapt fascination.

But then something happened to Kerouac. To everyone's surprise and embarrassment, the Pope of Zen started drinking too much. He became depressed and went to live with his mom. His marriages collapsed and his longtime friends were puzzled by his hostility. The movement that he sparked slowly faded out as later generations were lured away by the promise of respectability.

One lesson people drew from Kerouac's decline is that he had misunderstood Zen. Zen doesn't mean dropping out at all, but learning how to take each moment as it comes in a mindful, disciplined way. Zen means staying put, not freely wandering. We can't quit our jobs and head out for who knows where. Someone has to pay the rent and feed the kids. It's profoundly immature to think that freedom comes from abandoning our responsibilities. After the enlightenment, the dirty clothes remain and the kitchen sink still needs to be repaired.

Zen meditation—Zen practice itself—requires staying in one place. You don't live like the characters in *On the Road*, reciting free-form poetry throughout the night while you drink chianti with your wild friends. A Zen retreat will put you on your meditation mat for eight to ten hours every day.

Yet all the same, something was quite genuine about Kerouac's understanding of Zen. Staying put is part of the tradition, that's true, but so is a kind of outlaw wandering. According to the scholar and translator Red Pine, the most important Zen poet in Chinese is known to posterity as Han Shan, Cold Mountain. No other poet, Red Pine attests, enjoys the same preeminence. On "the altars of China's temples and shrines…his statue often stands" alone, a poet among immortals and enlightened beings.[145]

But Red Pine also adds a curious detail. To the mainstream Chinese intellectuals, Han Shan has always looked a bit déclassé—too rough, undisciplined, and unrefined. And for the Buddhist establishment as well, this crazy dropout seems not quite right, someone they don't want their monks and nuns to emulate, even though he's widely read and admired by people who think of him as *the* Zen poet.

Apparently Han Shan had held some kind of job in the ranks of government bureaucrats. And then, according to the legend anyway, he might have taken vows to become a monk. But just as he'd left the government behind, so he turned his back on the monastic way of life, choosing to stay on the mountain that became so much a part of him he took it as his name:

> Since I came to Cold Mountain
> how many years have passed
> accepting my fate I fled to the woods
> to dwell and gaze in freedom
> no one visits the cliffs
> forever hidden by clouds
> soft grass serves as a mattress
> my quilt is the dark blue sky
> a boulder makes a fine pillow
> Heaven and Earth can crumble and change.[146]

In the minds of many ordinary Chinese, Han Shan seemed to have realized the ideal celebrated by Taoist thinkers like Chuang Tzu—an existence of total spontaneity, unfolding in accord with nature's way. It's true that most readers of Han Shan's poetry didn't quit their jobs and go to dwell amid the clouds. They didn't want to rest their heads on rocks at night or shiver without a down coverlet. But Han Shan's poems still helped them recall another dimension of reality. Knowing that he lived in freedom, they could feel a little less trapped by the lives they led. Han Shan, at least, had escaped from history.

But isn't there a problem with this idea? When we say no to history—the collective dream made by our fellow human beings over many centuries—

aren't we saying no to this moment too, the moment that Zen teaches us to accept? In Zen we're told to shun the discriminating mind. "Make the smallest distinction," the great Seng T'san warned, "And heaven and earth are split...apart."[147] Didn't Han Shan split his world in two when he left behind the life down below? And haven't his admirers stumbled too when they look up from the endless round of chores and, sighing, dream of freedom in the mountains far away?

But Han Shan wasn't the only one who chose the outlaw's path of wandering. Almost a thousand years later in Japan, another restless spirit was destined become a beloved figure in the world of Zen. His name was Basho and these paragraphs are the first in his masterpiece *The Narrow Road to the Deep North*:

> Days and months are travelers of eternity. So are the years that pass by. Those who steer a boat across the sea, or drive a horse over the earth until they succumb to the weight of years, spend every minute of their lives traveling. There are a great number of ancients, too, who died on the road. I myself have been tempted for a long time by the cloud-moving wind—filled with a strong desire to wander.
>
> It was only towards the end of last autumn that I returned from rambling along the coast. I barely had time to sweep the cobwebs from my broken house on the River Sumida before the New Year, but no sooner had the spring mist begun to rise over the field than I wanted to be on the road again to cross the barrier-gate of *Shirakawa* in due time. The gods seemed to have possessed my soul and turned it inside out, and roadside images seemed to invite me from every corner, so that it was impossible for me to stay idle at home.[148]

"Cobwebs" is a poetic way for Basho to admit that his house wasn't clean. "Broken" means that it had become a wreck—a negligence unthinkable to most Japanese. He stayed there through the winter but the signs of spring sent him out on the road again in a pair of pants he mended for the trip. For him, traveling was crucial therapy. Nothing in his life had brought him happiness, even his fame as a brilliant poet. No sooner would he settle into a routine than he would start to grow depressed.

But on the road Basho could manage to break free from his expectations and perceive the timeless moments that he describes with such brilliance in his poetry:

> Along this road
> Goes no one;
> This autumn evening.[149]

Here we see the disappearance of the small self—the limited, ego-centered consciousness, clinging desperately to the usual routine. What replaces it is a greater "no one" that exists where time and the timeless intersect. Even though Basho is moving through time, he becomes a "traveler of eternity" like the days and months that pass while he's journeying. He's always going but he's always "here" as well. Each new moment brings him back to a "now" as complete as the one that preceded it. And yet, even though all of this is true, doesn't a problem still remain: like Han Shan, isn't Basho running away? Doesn't "being in the moment" seem to require that he should stay put and take his place in the world he shares with other human beings?

FOX ZEN

Perhaps not so surprisingly, there's a koan to address precisely this dilemma. It's known as the story of Hyakujo's fox.

In the eighth century Hyakujo was a Buddhist teacher held in high esteem. His talks on Zen practice were always packed with monks and lay people from all around his temple. And every time he spoke Hyakujo could see that an old man he didn't know would file in after the monks had sat down. Then, when the talk was over and the monks had left, the old man would quietly depart as well.

But one day the old man didn't leave. He came up to Hyakujo and introduced himself. "I am not a human being," he calmly declared. It turned out that the old man was actually a fox who could magically assume another form on occasions like the present one, when he wished to move unobtrusively in the realm of people.

Long, long ago he himself had been the head monk of a famous temple on the spot where Hyakujo's temple stood that day. And because the head monk was considered at that time a respected authority, he'd been approached by a younger monk who had put the following question to him: "Is an enlightened person still bound to cause and effect? Is he still caught in the dream of history? Or, after kensho, is he set free?"

Mistakenly, the head monk had replied, "Kensho definitely sets you free." And as karmic retribution for this mistake, the monk was reborn in the form of a fox, not just for one lifetime but possibly forever. So far he'd seen five hundred lives in a fox body.

And now, as he stood before Hyakujo, he said, "Brother monk, can you liberate me from my endless chain of fox rebirths? Can you tell me what I should have said?"

After the buildup of this amazing story, the answer given by Hyakujo ranks among the greatest letdowns of all time. In a reply that sounds like legalese with its evasive technicality, Hyakujo answers, "He does not ignore cause and effect."[150] In other words, he does not ignore the collective dream that is history.

But even though the answer seems dry and trite, somehow it magically does the trick. The fox gains enlightenment instantly. "Now," he says with joy, "I've finally been freed from my cycle of rebirths as a fox. I can die in peace and be buried here, on the very mountain where I lived long ago."

The fox story has so many elements taken from folk culture and Chinese myth that it might seem rather hard to penetrate. But when we sit with the koan for a while, we begin to recognize all the ways that we, too, would like to escape our next "rebirth." The timeless moments in our lives can be so beautiful that they make it all the harder to return to our unpleasant obligations and contingencies we simply can't control. Among monks and masters, this mentality is sometimes spoken of as "fox Zen"—wanting to hide in eternity while the world's troubles go rolling by. The koan seems to say that all of us are tempted by the same illusion that seduced the famous Zen runaways like Han Shan, Basho, and Kerouac. Even if we've found the time-less in the midst of time, we still want to run away from history.

When the head monk is asked about enlightenment, he basically says that if we're awake, we can turn our backs on whatever troubles us. But once we've learned the monk is reborn as a fox and we see how much he is suffering, we might think that he should have answered like this: "Don't be a fox—don't use Zen to run away! The enlightened person is never free, not from history or from anything else. Fit in, do your job, pay attention to details."

But as usual, there's another view. Things as they are can be unacceptable. It's easy to forget that until quite recently, people worked from dawn to dusk every day. The "day off" is a very recent idea, and so is the forty-hour week. Only a century ago, vacations were a new, contested idea. As with the health care debate today, these tiny spaces of liberty became a flash-point in a culture war. Powerful interests didn't want to concede control over time to the workers themselves. In fact, that was the message of the symbolic watch given to the worker on retirement day. Basically, the com-pany said to the old man, "Now we're giving your time back to you, after we've controlled it for last thirty years."

This puts another spin on things. There might be conditions we just shouldn't accept—moments when we have every right to declare, "I refuse to say yes to this. I'm prepared to quit or run away."

It's true in a certain sense that all moments hold the possibility of our awakening. And it's also true, just as Master Seng T'san says, that making even small distinctions cuts the world in two. Still, our readiness to embrace the status quo could be a bit like the Boy Scout Oath—expressing high ideals but at the price of a certain willful stupidity. Should we really wel-come every here and now as a destiny we're obligated to accept? Or is the matter really more complex?

POLEMICAL ZEN

It seems that the head monk in the koan on the fox fell into rebirth because he assumed that he could break free and live exactly as he pleased. Instead, he should have embraced his time and place—the reality he shared with others. But things aren't always as they seem. In the modern classic *Zen Mind, Beginner's Mind*, Shunryu Suzuki makes a few remarks about the way that we should live with history.

In particular, his remarks concern religion, the most compelling element of our collective dream—the one that holds in place the most basic architecture:

> Usually religion develops itself in the realm of consciousness, seeking to perfect its organization, building beautiful buildings, creating music, evolving a philosophy, and so forth. These are religious activities in the conscious world. But Buddhism emphasizes the world of unconsciousness.... The purpose of Buddhist teaching is to point to life itself existing beyond consciousness in our pure original mind.... In some ways Buddhism is rather polemical, with some feeling of controversy in it, because the Buddhist must protect his way from mystic or magical interpretations of religion.[151]

Words like "controversy" and "polemical" might come as a bit of a shock. Isn't Buddhist practice about "being peace"? Doesn't it require our acceptance of things? And yet Suzuki seems to think otherwise. The Zen he describes is at odds with religion, at least as we normally conceive of it.

We might suppose that the "mystic" and the "magical" are religion's beating heart, but Suzuki says this is quite untrue. No, these are the just products of the conscious mind, which uses words and ideas to represent a reality we experience more truthfully in a thoughtless and wordless way. The road to the unity that Zen opens up begins deep in the unconscious mind. In fact, the unity we find through Zen is one that the conscious mind can never fully grasp. The conscious mind has to quiet down and let the unconscious mind lead the way. And so Suzuki says that Zen should be "polemical." Its most important job is to stand apart from the contrivances the conscious mind has made. In a certain sense, Zen is always saying "no" to the collective dream of history.

The "mystic" and the "magical" are images of order. The world—the universe—is indeed orderly, but not in the way that consciousness thinks. Every time the conscious mind manages to invent an image of the world's unity, it forgets that images operate by simplifying what started out as complex. Suzuki says that Zen must resist this tendency. Zen has to show that the finger's not the moon: images of order aren't the order of things.

But rules are an image of order too—an image of how we should behave if we want to act in an orderly way. And if the job of Zen is polemical, then is it the way of Zen to obey the rules?

"Polemical" is a rather complicated word. It doesn't mean that you should tear the rulebook up, but neither does it mean that you should always obey. We needn't burn the temples down, shun the arts, and ignore philosophy. But our relation to them should be complex, and complex in a polemical way. As human beings we're equipped with conscious minds, and images are something we can't do without. Yet if we practice Zen we'll also understand that images, though necessary, aren't ever real.

Our problems begin, not only when we try to throw the rulebook out, but also when we work too hard to obey the imperfect rules that our history has made. We fall into the fox trap when we too willingly accept the architecture consciousness has built. The examples that Suzuki gives are from religion but they might have come from any area of culture—science, politics, and yes, even family life. Ideally, the temples, works of art, and the rest should serve the same purpose as the other buoys bobbling in the boundless ocean of the real, giving a helpful aura of permanence to what changes endlessly. But we tend to trust the buoys far too much.

The fox mind isn't just the one that urges us to phone in sick and watch tv all day. It's also the mind that wants good grades so much that we never ask if we like the course. It's the mentality of blue ribbon parents who won't give their kids an "unstructured" afternoon. The fox mind has taken hold when we're so concerned about appearances we go deep into debt just to buy a newer car.

Besides Suzuki, there's another man of Zen, a famous master in the T'ang dynasty, who made a point of being polemical. His name was Lin-chi (in Japanese, Rinzai), and here's what he said about obeying rules:

[In] past years [I] turned my attention to the *vinaya* [rules of con-
duct for monks], and I also delved into the sutras and treatises.
But later I realized that these are just medicines to cure the sickness of the world, expositions of surface matters. So finally I tossed
them aside and sought the Way through [Zen] practice....

Followers of the Way, if you want to get to the kind of understanding that accords with the Dharma, never be misled by others. Whether you're facing inward or facing outward, whatever
you meet up with, just kill it! If you meet a buddha, kill the
buddha. If you meet a patriarch, kill the patriarch.... If you meet
your parents, kill your parents. If you meet your kinfolk, kill your
kinfolk. Then for the first time you will gain emancipation, will
not be entangled with things, will pass freely anywhere you wish
to go.[152]

Of course, Lin-chi's words don't mean that we should ever do harm to any
living thing. Indeed, the kind of killing he instructs us to do might be the
only way that we can break free from our amazingly destructive way of life.

For Lin-chi, our basic predicament is that the force of history has grown
too great. This is what he means when he urges us to kill our parents and
our kin. The images of order that humanity has made have become more
and more encompassing. The irony is that the more trapped we feel, the
more energetically we try to get free by the very means that have bound us
tight, using words and ideas in a million ways with ever-greater skill and
elaboration.

Unlike many people in the West, Lin-chi sees progress is an illusion. He
wants his hearers to understand that long before the internet and TV, the
New York Times, and *People* magazine, long before Derrida and Wittgenstein,
Descartes, Plato, and the rest—and long before the God of Genesis too—
whatever humans are in essence was already fully present. The whole of history is a kind of fever dream, and unless we find a way of awakening, we'll
be smothered by the contrivances we falsely think have made us better
people.

At first it's hard to understand what Lin-chi could be thinking. Don't we all benefit from modern medicine, iPods, and computers? But Lin-chi doesn't want us to live in caves. We don't have to go back to the dawn of time. Instead he tells us that the dawn is always here—and that it's a wonderful place to be. When we stay with the moment for just a little while, we begin to see that our contrivances aren't as necessary as we believed—our CDs, the internet, the U.S. Treasury. With or without them, the perfection will be there, naturally perfect, requiring no effort. Of course it's possible that in antiquity humans acted badly, never bathed, and ate raw meat. But all the same, nothing can change the here and now, which was here and now for ancient humans too.

If we view the world through Lin-chi's eyes, we'll understand that what we call "civilization" has always been a kind of game we've played with a here and now that was perfect from the start. Everything that history has made—jet planes and public schools, stadiums and trucks—all of these are like the songs of birds or the flowering of a tree. The whole world that we've created out of time is really an expression of eternity. We sense this on occasion, often by surprise. Listening to music or looking at art, we'll suddenly appreciate its playful quality. Yet everything we make and do can have this playfulness. All of it's eternity in the flow of time.

But Lin-chi warns that we lose our way when we start to view our contrivances as essentials that we simply can't do without. Then we cling to them with ever growing desperation, imagining ourselves as fundamentally deficient. Because we fear our bodies are ugly underneath, we become slaves to the latest fashion trend. Unless we buy the most advanced technology, we'll be absurd and out of touch. Without deodorant our bodies will be vile; without education we'll be as dumb as the stones. Even though humans created history, this way of thinking turns the tables on us. It makes us feel inferior to images that have no reality apart from human beings. And once our images get the upper hand, we must kill the "Buddha" or be killed. Unless we overcome our subservience, something inside us will gradually die—the part that's the most spontaneous and alive.

MAD MONKS LIVING IN THE HILLS

How can we live with history but not get ensnared? How can we live in the collective dream but not be hypnotized by such a powerful illusion? The *Record of Lin-chi* makes it clear that this task will always be quite challenging.

Among the vignettes and teachings that comprise the *Record*, a number of them tell of a wild monk who was named P'u-hua. Although Lin-chi himself was widely known for his polemical attitude, P'u-hua outdid him in every way. Always dirty, P'u-hua dressed in tattered robes. He wandered the streets like a Shakespearean fool, uttering nonsense to anyone who'd listen. Among the villagers P'u-hua had become a source of amusement and something else as well—P'u-hua was so heedless of the normal rules that he made the town a little nervous.

In the stories where P'u-hua and Lin-chi interact, P'u-hua always goes too far. On one occasion a villager had invited them to his family's home for a vegetarian meal. In the Chinese Buddhism of the time, honoring monks with a banquet this way had become a standard form of *dana* or gift-giving. For their part, the monks were expected to repay the giver with a private instruction of some kind.

In keeping with the rules, Lin-chi and P'u-hua went to the banquet where they ate quietly for a while. And then, at a moment that seemed appropriate, Lin-chi began teaching just as he'd planned, starting with this koan: "One hair swallows up the huge sea; one mustard seed holds Mount Sumeru. Is this a manifestation of supernatural power, or the way things have always been?"[153]

The question draws on the Vimalakirti Sutra where the great bodhisattva uses his power to pack a multitude of the Buddha's followers into the dimensions of a tiny room. The ocean can now fit on a single strand of hair. A mustard seed can contain Mount Sumeru, which embodies the entire universe.[154] Was this, Lin-chi asks, a miraculous event, or are space and time truly relative?

As koans go, this one is quite accessible, and it's likely that the host knew the sutra well. Maybe it was Lin-chi's plan to give his listeners a taste of how koan training actually works. Perhaps he meant to follow the question with a lesson on the practice of zazen—how to make the conscious mind grow more still, and then how to internalize the koan in a way that allows the unconscious mind to do its work. Or possibly he meant to test the layman's depth—maybe this was someone who'd been practicing under Lin-chi's guidance for many years.

Meals and banquets played a crucial role in helping to maintain close relationships between monks or nuns and the communities they served. The story implies that Lin-chi was quite adept at managing events of this important kind. He had all the necessary social skills. He knew how to behave in polite society and was an accomplished raconteur who always grasped what to say and when. Monks and nuns who were incompetent wouldn't have been authorized to leave the temple grounds, or, as in P'u-hua's own case, they would have been expected to keep still.

But alas, this is not what P'u-hua did. No sooner had Lin-chi's question been posed then P'u-hua lurched explosively, sending bowls and chopsticks flying everywhere. The banquet table now lay in utter disarray. The layman and his family were shocked and distressed, and the opportunity to teach was lost.

"Too coarse," the master yelled across the table to P'u-hua, scolding him for his wild ways.

To which P'u-hua answered, "Where do you think you are, talking about what's coarse and fine? We both know that your distinction is unreal."

The story itself is a koan that explores the proper way to live in a world where we need contrivances that are illusory. Probably the layman and his family were motivated by the best intentions. For their generosity they deserved more than noodles splattered on the floor and stained tablecloths. But in the stories where P'u-hua appears, something like this disaster often takes place.

At certain moments Lin-chi seems to look with suspicion on his fellow monk, as though he can never quite decide if he's enlightened or simply mad. But if that's true, then why did he bring P'u-hua when he went to the house that day? Maybe Lin-chi was a poor judge of character—and not at all what he was cracked up to be. But possibly he had something up his sleeve. P'u-hua goes too far—that's clearly true. Yet the *Record of Lin-chi* also seems to show that he deeply understands the real nature of things. Of the many people in the book, it's actually P'u-hua who demonstrates the most profound enlightenment.

HISTORY AND NAKEDNESS

But all the same, there's something about P'u-hua that readers might find intimidating or worse. Who would want to train under a master like him? Would you trust a parent who behaved that way, or a crazy but enlightened boss?

Pu-hua's problem is one we can't escape as easily as we might prefer. In fact, if we continue to practice Zen, it's a koan each of us will have to resolve at some moment of our lives. The myth of history has gained such unchallenged power because it claims to shelter us from the groundlessness that P'u-hua embraced without any conditions. And so those of us who practice Zen will have to face one obstacle no matter what we do: the fear that we'll become as strange and scary as P'u-hua—or the ultimate outsider like Jack Kerouac.

Yet the *Record of Lin-chi* drops a number of hints that its namesake needed P'u-hua's help in order to become the great Zen master that he did. Even though it's true that Lin-chi often maintains a certain distance from his wild counterpart, most of the time it appears to be an act. They seem to relish each other's company—the respected master and the lunatic.

But in the West, history is all about casting out that crazy monk— ancient, uncouth, uninstructed, unredeemed, a throwback to humans long ago. In order to fabricate the collective dream of our eventual deliverance, it was first essential to create the idea of that man's defectiveness. And so we see the real engine of history. It wasn't the hunger for knowledge or truth, or even for security. The engine of history has always been shame:

> And the eyes of [Adam and Eve] were opened, and they knew
> that they were naked; and they sewed fig leaves together, and
> made themselves aprons. And they heard the voice of the Lord
> God walking in the garden in the cool of the day: and Adam and
> his wife hid themselves from the presence of the Lord God

amongst the trees of the garden. And the Lord God called unto Adam, and said unto him, Where art thou? And he said, I heard thy voice in the garden, and I was afraid, because I was naked; and I hid myself. And he said, Who told thee that thou wast naked? Hast thou eaten of the tree, whereof I commanded thee that thou shouldest not eat?[155]

With this scene, Western history begins. From this moment on until the end of time, shame is to be our inescapable fate.

Genesis makes an unforgettable point. The mark of our confusion is not our nakedness but the need we feel to hide ourselves beneath clothes. And yet after the Fall it is this nakedness that becomes the sign of our total defeat—a loss of natural innocence we'll never regain for as long as this earth continues to exist.

But anyone who's practiced Zen meditation, even for a little while, knows that this thinking is upside down. What we are essentially is nothing at all, and when we embrace that emptiness, everything around us becomes new and alive. Everything becomes, as we say, the true self. But in the split second we deny this emptiness, God is banished and Eden withers away.

In Zen we don't wear robes to conceal our shame. We wear them to protect our real innocence—the eternity at the heart of time. Even though no one can control history, each of us can bring the timeless into our lives. Each of us can make a place for P'u-hua, even if that means we'll have to live between two worlds, the collective dream and the here and now. Is P'u-hua monstrous or beautiful, ancient or ageless, holy or profane? However we describe him, such words are just the robes. And the robes, no matter how skillfully made, are destined to end up like the rags he wore. But this—this moment—won't ever wear out.

In fact, it's always at the beginning again.

CONCLUSION:
BUDDHA AT THE APOCALYPSE

Buddha at the Apocalypse—how exactly would that look? If the world really were about to end, what would the Buddha do?

Would he watch serenely as the moon turned blood red and the stars tumbled from the sky? Would he close his eyes as Sin and Death wasted a fourth of humankind?

Or, what would happen if the End conformed to the Buddhist predictions instead? What if one destruction were to follow the next in a terrifying spiral? Would the Buddha enter deep samadhi and ascend into meditation heaven where he'd go unscathed?

To contemplate the end of absolutely everything might inspire terror, or, perhaps for some, relief. But the questions we've just posed each depend on assumptions people tend to overlook. When we ask, for instance, how the world will end, we're assuming that it has to end at all. And that assumption rests on another one, which might prove even more dubious. We're assuming that the world began long ago—and that it actually exists right now. The truth is that neither of these beliefs might be justified by a reality more complex than either one.

Admittedly, it seems self-evident that if anything exists, it must have had a beginning of some kind. And beginnings can't exist without endings too. And these two imply some sort of middle as well. Ever since we were little kids, we've learned this lesson again and again.

At some point most of us have enjoyed the pleasure of a roaring fire— not the one that's going to consume the earth, but the one we build in the fireplace. To prepare, we could gather twigs and chop some wood, which we'd arrange, more or less skillfully. First there's the moment when we strike the match and hold it to the paper underneath the twigs. The paper takes the flame and ignites the twigs, which ignite the larger sticks and, finally, the logs. The logs burn fiercely for quite a while, radiating their delicious warmth and light, but gradually the fire consumes the fuel, cooling down and going dark.

The whole sequence has a clear trajectory from the beginning to the middle to the end. Of course, fires aren't the only events that are thought to unfold in this sequential way. Every event appears to do the same. And so it seems quite natural to scale it up: the universe itself must be moving through time just like the modest little fire we made. There must have been a moment like our gathering the twigs. There must be a moment when it all burns bright, followed by a moment when it all goes out. In the case of the fire, the process seems so clear that no one would ever think to question it. A camcorder might capture the whole event. If anybody doubted us, we could play the sequence back, settling the matter right then and there.

And yet in his writings Master Dogen makes an utterly outlandish claim. He says that the ashes in the fireplace have no direct connection to the firewood.[156] If Dogen were just an ordinary monk, hardly anyone would pay him any mind. But so many people have been impressed by his extraordinary depth that they try to cut him a little slack even though he often leaves them scratching their heads. This time, though, his point seems beyond belief—unless you've done a fair amount of meditation.

If you've been practicing Zen for a while, you might have noticed a change that eventually becomes quite predictable. When you've entered into deep concentration, every moment seems to be self-contained. It's as though the here and now is all that exists. Past and future don't completely disappear, but they appear to recede subtly—becoming the past and future of this single moment. This must be what Dogen had in mind in his comments on the firewood and what remains when the fire's gone out. When we pay attention to reality with a different sort of intelligence, we notice what ordinary consciousness can't. The small mind, the conscious mind, prefers a time that flows, but Dogen argues that this flowing time isn't the entire story. Another dimension exists, as we've seen, a timelessness that doesn't move. In the moment of the burning wood, there's burning wood and only that. The moment of ashes is ashes through and through.

Even if you haven't ever practiced Zen, this reasoning makes a certain sense. Each moment might indeed be all that exists—at that moment anyway. But even if we're willing to accept this argument, there's still something that doesn't quite add up. If each moment is a totality, what exists between the totalities? There's the eternal here and now of the raging fire. And then there's the here and now of the cold, gray ashes. But what lies in between the two? "Nothing" is the answer Dogen would give, but he wouldn't mean what you might think.

SOMETHING AND NOTHING

For a moment—if "a moment" actually exists—let's imagine ourselves sitting once again in a darkened theater. We're watching the movie and having a great time. The hero is just about to kiss the leading lady. Their eyes meet, their faces are drawing near, but just then the spectacle on the screen begins flickering and breaking up. Now the beautiful illusion is gone. Instead of one continuous flow, what we see are discrete images, like a series of still photographs rather than a moving picture. Finally the images come to a stop and somebody switches on the lights. Something's gone wrong with the projector, they announce.

The truth is that all we ever see on the screen are individual images. But our minds supply a continuity that the images don't possess. Between each image and the next, there is really an empty space that our minds want us to ignore, and the projector helps us out by firing the images very rapidly. Except on those occasions when things go wrong, we only notice the continuity, the seamless flow that we help to create. But when the projector gets out of sync, we can plainly see the static images, and we can observe the empty spaces in between.

If you do zazen long enough, you will experience this empty space between the moments when the world seems to exist in a timeless, changeless way. The Japanese word for this space is "Mu," which means, quite simply, "nothing" or "emptiness." Finding Mu might take you a few months or it could require several years, but if you focus your attention on anything, you'll eventually bump into Mu. The object of attention might be your breath, gently going in and out, or the rhythmic sound of the crickets outside, or a candle on the floor in front of you, or an image that you visualize. But no matter what you focus on, sooner or later it will lead you to the space where absolutely nothing exists. The first time you become aware of this space, it might seem to pass by in a flash. You might even wonder if anything occurred. But gradually the empty spaces will acquire a longer duration and a kind of depth, like an ocean you are swimming in at night.

Zen teachers have a penchant for the dramatic. Over the centuries when they've tried to describe what Mu or emptiness is like, they've spoken of it as a kind of death. "Die on the cushion!" they frequently shout. The death they have in mind might be just a metaphor, but they could mean it quite literally. Maybe those empty moments are indeed where we'll wind up when our lives reach the end. Or maybe they're just a trick played by our minds, an odd defect of human consciousness.

But that wouldn't be what most Buddhists think. The bodhisattva Avalokiteshvara—the one known in Chinese as Kwan-yin—describes Mu this way in the Heart Sutra, probably the most important sutra in Zen:

In emptiness [we find] no form, no feelings, perceptions, impulses, consciousness. No eyes, no ears, no nose, no tongue, no body, no mind; no color, no sound, no smell, no taste, no touch, no object of mind; no realm of eyes and so forth until no realm of mind consciousness. No ignorance and also no extinction of it, and so forth until no old age and death and also no extinction of them. No suffering, no origination, no stopping, no path, no cognition, also no attainment with nothing to attain.[157]

Avalokiteshvara doesn't say that nothingness is just an illusion or a fluke in the design of human brain. He, or she—the bodhisattva can be both—says it's the basic reality.

If you're willing to concede that this might indeed be possible, the implications could seem rather frightening. In the West, we often think of emptiness or nothingness as the occasion for deep despair. If life really is One Big Nothingness, then why should we take the trouble to go on? Total nothingness could sound even worse than an eternity in the Christian hell, since you would at least still exist, and possibly God might change his mind. Nothingness could be worse than hell itself!

But the sutra goes on to say something else: the experience of emptiness ends all suffering.[158] Emptiness is a sure way out of hell. And this is indeed what Zen students learn. Even if this emptiness looks a lot like death, or like the world coming to an end, its effect on our lives is astonishing. It can free you from every fear. There's no memory, habit, or buried trauma—no obstacle of any kind—that it can't dissolve like water wearing down a stone.

Mu doesn't liberate by transforming what exists through some special kind of alchemy. The nature of things doesn't change at all. What has changed is our perception of them. We discover that everything is Mu, and that Mu is everything. "Form is emptiness," the sutra declares, "emptiness is form." And when we see our obstacles for what they are—fundamentally nothingness—their hold over us gradually erodes.

Form and emptiness are believed to be different aspects of the same reality. They're not even different sides of the same coin. They're like different views of the same thing. The seventeenth-century master Hakuin wrote that the difference between enlightened mind and our ordinary consciousness is like the difference between water and ice. Ice is always water fundamentally, but it seems like another substance when the temperature drops below the freezing point.[159]

The *thingness* of things shouldn't be ignored—the *rockness* of rocks, the *treeness* of trees—even if the rocks and trees are always more than such words can ever express. If we simply dismiss it all as an illusion, we aren't doing justice to reality. The sutra doesn't teach that there's no form at all. Hakuin didn't tell us that ice doesn't exist. But in a way the conscious mind can't quite understand, Mu—nothingness—is also everything.

All of this puts in a rather different light the question of where the Buddha might go when the Apocalypse arrives. To say, as the Book of Revelation does, that the world exists and then, at some point, it will all abruptly end—that might be a bit too neat. Even the Buddhist cosmology might not be complex enough. True, it tells us the universe will start again once it's been nearly destroyed. But the reality might not correspond to that account of things either. It's not as though nothingness just disappears for a maha kalpa and then comes back just in time to wrap things up. Dogen, Hakuin, and the Heart Sutra think it's always present in some way.

But what way, exactly, would that be? How can everything and nothing coexist? That's pretty hard to wrap your mind around.

There's a koan that might help to clarify the matter. On one occasion when he was young, a Chinese master of long ago had the chance to meet the great Joshu, who was then many years his senior. And when they met, Joshu asked him this: "What if a person of the Great Death comes back to life again?"

The phrase Great Death might be understood as nothingness itself. And so the koan could be taken to mean, "Once everything has completely disappeared, once you yourself are only emptiness, what will happen then, if anything?"

In response the younger master gave this reply: "Don't go by night; wait for the light of day to come."[160] As usual with koans, this answer might seem to make very little sense. But if you've spent a lot of time in Mu, sooner or later you will observe that you can't stay forever in that empty space even though it's so profoundly liberating. No matter how deeply you concentrate, something is going to interrupt your beautiful, untrammeled emptiness.

The universe always comes back again. No matter how skillfully we meditate, emptiness won't stay empty for very long. Something always seems to keep popping up.

If your goal is to stay in Mu without breaks or interruptions, this oscillation will appear to pose an enormous problem. But if you stop assuming there's something wrong, you can sit back and enjoy the show, knowing it's the way things have to be. The oscillation is the natural order of things. In fact, it can't be stopped no matter what we do.

THE INDESTRUCTIBILITY OF IMPERMANENCE

As it turns out, our universe is rather difficult to kill. No matter how thoroughly it disappears into total nothingness, the whole thing just keeps coming back.

But what are the implications of that? Doesn't it suggest that we'll get off scot-free? We can trash the planet at no cost to ourselves, since the universe is always sure to return. Talk about disposability!

Even if this whole world should disappear, the story won't have ended there. The world will come back and when it does, so will the reverberations from our past deeds—reverberations like the ripples we produce when we throw a pebble into a lake. And these reverberations will help create events we'll have to deal with at the time of our rebirth. "Rebirth" can simply be understood as a metaphor, or we can take it quite literally. But either way, it implies a continuity—from one wave to wave, from life to life, or from one universe to the next. This is Karma 101.

Often when the Buddha mentioned karma, he spoke of it in the context of rebirth. But rebirth is never described as an event that involves an isolated individual. It always happens in the context of a world for which that person is responsible. A person whose actions are "afflictive," causing harm, will be reborn in an "afflictive world." By contrast, the person whose karma is "bright" will be reborn in a "non-afflictive world," or possibly in a "heavenly realm" of perfect but temporary happiness.[161] Even higher than the heavenly realm would be the state of enlightenment, which has karmic roots in the generosity of selfless service to others. Enlightenment starts with our actions in the world, and it will lead back there as well. The Buddha, after all, didn't turn away from us. He knew that one wave will always follow the next, and he tried to set in motion a wave so deep that it would lift countless other beings.

The basis of Zen's ecology of mind is an understanding of this connectedness—a connectedness that reaches across time. In a certain sense, every moment is new—a new start for the whole universe. And all of our nows are like the ashes and the wood, self-contained eternities. Yet it's also true that wave leads to wave. The reverberations of yesterday's deeds will carry over to this day, and even the gods in highest heaven lack the power to undo what we set in motion now. Zen's ecology of mind starts right here: we can't wait until tomorrow. The future can't undo what we do here—not even with the best new technology. Our only hope is acting mindfully today. That's the lesson old Zuigan tried to impart to his young unsui when he declared, "There's no such thing as trash!"

THE THEOLOGY OF POSTPONEMENT

For two thousand years people in the West have been preparing for the end of time. Even if we hold the notion loosely in our minds, we still believe that some moment yet to come holds the key to everything. Some point in the future will make it all clear, and so, the future is where we have to go. In no other way will we ever understand who we really are or what this life is all about.

As for the fundamentalists, their way of thinking is more...fundamental. Most of them believe what Revelation teaches: the earth will be destroyed and reborn again, but now without the death and sin. Those who have rejected Christ will burn eternally. Those who have been saved will live happily forever. It's written in the scriptures and that how it's going to be.

Needless to say, followers of the Buddha would have a lot of trouble with much of this. But the major sticking point wouldn't be the angels or the rain of fire. It wouldn't even be the eternity in hell, even though that sounds rather challenging and might require a lot of meditation. No, the basic sticking point would have to be the way of life this view of time implies. From the polemical perspective of Zen, living for the future isn't living skillfully. In fact, it's destructive in many ways that we ignore to our detriment.

When the West looks back at itself, it often does so in the spirit of congratulation. And one of the virtues it loves to celebrate is its dynamism. Living for the future has made the West open to every form of change. Moving forward faster than anyone, it has gained the wealth and power it deserves.

Admittedly, this argument carries some real weight, but there's another way to see the West and the way of life it has created. The same culture that we could describe as so adept at getting things done might be seen as profoundly escapist. The West, which prides itself on being down to earth and prepared for anything, has a hard time with reality. That's because our civilization has been built on a refusal to address the consequences of what we do. Instead, we've made an entire way of life based on the habit of postponement. And now that our influence has spread globally, our habit of postponement has been exported too.

Today many millions of us are engaged in activities that entail enormous risk to all terrestrial life. Certain labs here in the United States have made substances so dangerous that a few drops in the public water system could wipe out our major cities. Thousands of tons of nuclear waste lie exposed to the cold and rain, their containers rusting while the federal government wrangles with state governors over storage sites. But when it comes to dangers that threaten life, there are countless other sources as well. Industries make so many new chemicals that oversight has become impossible. No one even knows how many we've created, or what the long-term consequences might turn out to be. At the same time, genetic science has given us the ability to gamble recklessly with the components of our cells as well as the cells of the food we eat. And, of course, there's still a somewhat older threat: an unknown number of world states that maintain arsenals of nuclear missiles.

These threats aren't secrets. They're widely known. But why isn't anybody doing anything? Many explanations would help to shed some light, and no single one would account for everything. Yet surely any list of the reasons should include our culture's blind faith in the world to come, in both its secular and religious forms. Because that blind faith is so integrally a part of the way we've been raised to think, we tend to discount its significance. Yet that's how all mental architecture works, structuring experience pervasively but in a way that passes unnoticed.

It has to matter enormously that the founding documents of our civilization promise that the future will be better than the past. Utopia or the New Jerusalem, one or the other is our destiny. And so it makes a great deal of sense that we tend to leave the most urgent tasks undone—overseeing the nuclear waste, taking the warheads out of commission, curbing our outputs of carbon dioxide.

It might be revealing to think of the future as what biologists refer to as a "commons." The word comes from European history and it refers to the pastureland collectively owned by the residents of medieval farming towns. The commons were the shared property of every village, and all the villagers could graze livestock there. If everybody used the land with some regard for the needs of everyone else, the story of the commons would have had a happy ending. But in the field of biology, scientists sadly noted what they call "the tragedy of the commons." Some villagers always put their self-interest far ahead of the common good. A wily farmer might use the shared pastureland until the grass was nearly gone, and then he'd leave the cost of bringing it back to health for the whole community to bear later on. This is exactly how we treat the future now. The future is our commons and almost everyone leaves the mess for some hapless future generation.[162]

Our neglect of the mess is not a rational response, nor is it a natural one in any way. In fact, it's the very opposite of both.

As we've seen, our behavior has been shaped by our culture's past. Through the stories people hear in growing up, through family life, the media, formal education, and most of all, through religion, we've internalized the mentality of waiting for the future to save us. Postponement has become habitual. In fact, it's an article of religious faith.

But the Dharma teaches us that humans are endowed with a most fortunate trait. They have the ability to change themselves, while accepting things as they really are, perfect in their way, and imperfect too. Even though we're addicted to the future tense, we can still start to live in a different way.

We can still learn to live attentively in the here and now.

It might be the ultimate paradox that trusting the moment actually depends on the experience of emptiness. Being in the here and now doesn't mean trying to hold on with an iron grip to what is actually happening. Instead it's a matter of letting go. When we can't be in the here and now, it's because we don't know how to extricate ourselves from our dreams about a better future world. But when we see the moment through the eyes of Mu, we can let events unfold naturally without trying to control or interfere. To see the world this way is to look impartially. It's like watching the moon in a lake at night, or the smoke rising from an incense stick, or the path of birds flying in the air—this is how the sutras tell us it will be. When we see things as they really are, we understand that they're impermanent, and, indeed, that we're impermanent too.

People might assume that taking this to heart would mean no longer caring about anything. "Why would it matter," goes this reasoning, "if we poison the water, let the forests die, or watch as millions of our fellow human beings grind along in sickness and poverty?" Since nothing lasts forever, why should we care?

Yet it's often the case that the things we love become more precious when we're just about to leave.

Once this impermanence hits you between the eyes, everything looks completely different. You enter a condition that you'll never understand—and you know it really is one great life, just as Gempo Roshi said. You can try to describe it, but you can't succeed. The very words you reach for are destined to wear out, and only half-truths for as long as they last.

The river we call time is unstoppable, but when we unify ourselves with the here and now, there's no longer a beginning or an end.

Perhaps this is what the nun Xinggang meant to say in the poem with which this book began. If the Apocalypse should someday come, where will we find the Buddha?

A single meditation cushion, and one is completely protected,
Earth may crumble, heaven collapse—but here one is at peace.[163]

NOTES

INTRODUCTION

1 Nancy Gibbs, "Apocalypse Now," *Time Magazine*, 23 June 2002, www.time.com/time/covers/1101020701/story.html. See also Paul Boyer, *When Time Shall Be No More: Prophecy Belief in Modern American Culture* (Cambridge: Belknap/Harvard University Press, 1992).

2 Robert Dreyfus, "Reverend Doomsday," *Rolling Stone*, 28 January 2004, www.rollingstone.com/politics/story/5939999/reverend_doomsday/.

3 See Chip Berlet and Nakhil Aziz, "Culture, Religion, Apocalypse, and Middle East Foreign Policy," *Right Web*, 5 December 2003, rightweb.irc-online.org/rw/848.html; Paul S. Boyer, "The Iraq War Mets Biblical Prophecy," *Albion Monitor*, 23 February 2003, www.albionmonitor.com/0302a/iraqbible.html; Charles Marsh, "Wayward Christian Soldiers," *New York Times*, 20 January 2006, www.nytimes.com/2006/01/20/opinion/20marsh.html; Chris Hedges, *American Fascists: The Christian Right and the War on America* (New York: Free Press, 2006), esp. 182–87.

4 See Max Blumenthal, "Birth Pangs of a New Christian Zionism," *The Nation*, 8 August 2006, www.thenation.com/doc/20060814/new_christian_zionism, and Bill Moyers, "Christians United for Israel (CUFI)," *Bill Moyers' Journal*, 7 October 2007, www.pbs.org/moyers/journal/10052007/profile.html.

5 See Bruce Wilson, "New Army Chaplain Thinks He's 'Chosen by God,' Predicts Apocalyptic Religious War," *Alternet.org*, 9 August 2007,

www.alternet.org/blogs/peek/59273/new_army_head_of_chaplains_
thinks_he's_%22chosen_by_god%22,_predicts_apocalyptic_religious_
war/. See also Max Blumenthal, "Pentagon Sends Messengers of Apocalypse to Convert Christian Soldiers in Iraq," *Alternet.org*, 8 August 2007,
www.alternet.org/waroniraq/59161/.

6   Jerry Falwell, "The Myth of Global Warming" (sermon), Thomas Road
Baptist Church, Lynchburg, VA, 25 February 2007. Quoted in Bob
Allen, "Falwell Says Global Warming Tool of Satan," *EthicsDaily.com*, 3
January 2007, www.ethicsdaily.com/news.php?viewStory=8596.

7   Arianna Huffington, "The Pentagon Sounds the Alarm on Global
Warming; Why Isn't President Bush Listening," *CommonDreams.org*, 25
February 2004, www.commondreams.org/views04/0225-13.htm.

8   Isaiah 58:11. The Holy Bible, New International Version [NIV] (Grand
Rapids: Zondervan Publishers, 1984). For centuries Christian theologians have read the prophetic books "backward," especially Isaiah and
Daniel, in order to find "prior" confirmation for the Christian view of
eschatology. This anachronism distorts the meaning of the Jewish Bible.
See S. Talmon, "The Concepts of Māšîah and Messianism in Early
Judaism," in *The Messiah: Developments in Earliest Judaism and Christi-
anity*, ed. James H. Charlesworth (Minneapolis: Fortress Press, 1992),
79–115; Jacob Neusner, "Messianic Themes in Formative Judaism," *Journal of the American Academy of Religion* 52: 2 (1984): 357–74; and David
Klinghoffer, *Why the Jews Rejected Jesus: The Turning Point in Western
History* (New York: Doubleday, 2005), esp. 33–71.

9   Some of the early classics in this field are still well worth reading. See
James Gleick, *Chaos: The Making of a New Science* (New York: Penguin,
1988); Stuart Kauffman, *At Home in the Universe: The Search for Laws
of Self-Organization and Complexity* (New York: Oxford University Press,
1996); M. Mitchell Waldrop, *Complexity: The Emerging Science at the
Edge of Order and Chaos* (New York: Simon and Schuster, 1992); and
John H. Holland, *Emergence: From Chaos to Order* (New York: Basic
Books, 1999).

10 The teaching of the Rapture holds that just before the tribulations of the
Apocalypse, the saved will be "taken up into the air" where they will be

with Jesus. This teaching is rejected as un-Biblical by the Catholic Church, the Greek Orthodox Church, and all mainline Protestant denominations. Most Evangelicals accept it, including Tim LaHaye and Jerry Jenkins. Indeed, they see the Rapture as *the* decisive moment in world history.

11   This is a modern-English rendering of Case 5, "Kyogen's Man Up a Tree," in the *Mumonkan*. See *Gateless Gate*, www.sacred-texts.com/bud/zen/mumonkan.htm.

12   "The test of a first-rate intelligence is the ability to hold two opposed ideas in the mind at the same time, and still retain the ability to function." F. Scott Fitzgerald, "The Crack-up," in *The Crack-up, with Other Uncollected Pieces, Notebooks and Unpublished Letters* (New York: J. Laughlin, 1962), 69.

13   For the term "ecology of mind" as well as the idea, I am indebted to Gregory Bateson, *Steps to an Ecology of Mind: Collected Essays in Anthropology, Psychiatry, Evolution, and Epistemology* (Chicago: University of Chicago Press, 2000).

14   Soko Morinaga, *Novice to Master*, trans. Belinda Attaway Yamakawa (Boston: Wisdom Publications, 2004), 27–31.

CHAPTER 1

15   Genesis 1:1–4 (NIV).

16   Genesis 1:21–22 (King James Version [KJV]).

17   Genesis 1:28 (KJV).

18   Genesis 2:21–23.

19   Genesis 3.

20   Genesis 4:12 (American Standard Version).

21   Genesis 6:5–7 (KJV).

22   Genesis 6–9 (NIV).

23   Exodus 11:5 (KJV), 14.

24   Augustine, *Reply to Faustus the Manichaean*, VII.70–78. www.ccel.org/ccel/schaff/npnf104.iv.ix.xxiv.html.

25   Exodus 15:3 (KJV).

26   Exodus 15:14–16 (NIV).

27   Isaiah 65:17; 2 Peter 3:13 (NIV).

28   Isaiah 66:12 (KJV).

29   Isaiah 66:15–20 (New King James Version). See also Gershom Scholem, *The Messianic Idea in Judaism* (New York: Schocken Books, 1971), 1–36. As Scholem writes, "Hosea, Amos, [and] Isaiah know only a single world, in which even the End of Days run their course. Their eschatology is of a national kind: it speaks of the reestablishment of the house of David" (6). It does not speak of "a new heaven and a new earth."

30   Luke 15:11–32.

31   Luke 15:17 (KJV).

32   Luke 15:21 (KJV).

33   Luke 15:29–30 (KJV).

34   Luke 15:31–32 (KJV).

35   Both passages NIV.

36   John 2:15–16 (KJV).

37   Matthew 13:36–43 (NIV).

38   KJV.

39   A key source here is René Girard, *Things Hidden Since the Foundation of the World*, trans. Stephen Bann and Michael Meteer (London: Athlone Press, 1987). Girard, however, takes the view that Christianity rejects the logic of the scapegoat—the logic of blood atonement. Although his exploration of violence and the sacred is enormously revealing, this assertion seems to fly directly in the face of the scriptural evidence as well as two thousand years of Biblical exegesis.

40   When he was busy with his German translation of the Bible, working from a Greek version, Luther had mixed feelings about including the Book of Revelation. In a preface to his first translation, he expressed these feelings openly. He said that he doubted the book's authenticity. "First and foremost," he wrote, "it is not the way of the apostles to recount visions, but to prophecy in clear and simple words; this is done by St. Peter and St. Paul, and by Christ in the gospels.... I cannot imagine that [Revelation] owes its existence to the Holy Spirit." *Reformation Writings of Martin Luther*, Vol. II, *The Spirit of the Protestant Reformation*, trans. Bertram Lee Woolf (London: Lutterworth Press, 1956), 309.

41   Revelation 1:13–18 (KJV).

42   Revelation 6:8 (NIV).

43   Revelation 6:12–13 (KJV).

44   Revelation 22:13 (NIV).

45   "Teaching: Prophecy and Babylon," *PatRobertson.com*, 2005, www. patrobertson.com/Teaching/TeachingonBabylon.asp.

46   *Paul Zahn Now*, 24 July 2006, CNN.com Transcripts, transcripts.cnn. com/TRANSCRIPTS/0607/24/pzn.01.html.

CHAPTER 2

47   Luke 12:22–31 (NIV).

48   Luke: 12:33–34 (NIV). See also Matthew 6:25–33.

49   St. Eucherius of Lyon, *De Contemptu Mundi* (1645 Henry Vaughan translation), *Christian Classics Ethereal Library*, www.ccel.org/ccel/ eucherius/contempt.txt.

50   See Mark 9:1, Matthew 16:28, Luke 9:26–27, Matthew 24:34.

51   Martin Luther, *The Freedom of a Christian*, in *Martin Luther's Basic Theological Writings* (Minneapolis: Fortress Press, 1989), 585–629, at 596, 606–7.

52   Martin Luther, *Commentary on the Epistle to the Galatians* (1535), trans. Theodore Graebner (Grand Rapids: Zondervan Publishing House, 1949), 86–106. Project Wittenberg, www.iclnet.org/pub/resources/ text/wittenberg/luther/gal/web/gal3-01.html.

53   See Boyer, *When Time Shall Be No More*, 68–79.

54   John Winthrop, "A Model of Christian Charity," *Religious Freedom*, religiousfreedom.lib.virginia.edu/sacred/charity.html.

55   William Ames, "The End of the World," *A Puritan's Mind*, www.apuritansmind.com/William%20Ames/WilliamAmesEndOf TheWorld.htm.

56   "Of Good Works," *The Westminster Confession of Faith*, Center for Reformed Theology and Apologetics, www.reformed.org/documents/ wcf_with_proofs/.

As the *Confession* says of people who do good works, "Their ability...is not at all of themselves, but wholly from the Spirit of Christ. And that they may be enabled thereunto, beside the graces they have already received, there is required an actual influence of the same Holy Spirit, to work in them to will, and to do, of His good pleasure" (XVI:III).

57   Quoted in John E. Smith, "Jonathan Edwards: Piety and Practice in the American Character," *Journal of Religion* 54:2 (April 1974): 166–80, at 176.

58   Jonathan Edwards, "Sinners in the Hands of an Angry God," in *Sermons and Discourses, 1739–1742* (WJE Online Vol. 22), ed. Harry S. Stout, *The Jonathan Edwards Center at Yale University*, edwards.yale.edu/research/major-works/sinners-in-the-hands-of-an-angry-god/.

59   See Robert J. Barro and Rachel M. McCleary, "Religion and Economic Growth," Harvard University, 8 April 2003, www.economics.harvard.edu/faculty/barro/files/Religion_and_Economic_Growth.pdf.

60   Michelle Boorstein reports on a 2006 Baylor University survey of religious attitudes in "Americans May Be More Religious Than They Realize," *Washington Post*, 12 September 2006, www.washingtonpost.com/wp-dyn/content/article/2006/09/11/AR2006091100459.html.

61   Of course no thinker does it all by himself. No thinker starts from scratch and operates in a vacuum, unaffected by others. Yet some people play a special role. In a figure like Hegel, the vectors of culture intersect in a way that exerts disproportionate force, perhaps unexpectedly. If cultures too are complex systems, then some ideas can precipitate a major change of direction, like the first grain of sand whose motion shifts the whole pile, or the first molecule to cross a fluid barrier, followed by a torrent of others. Hegel was this kind of thinker.

62   See Georg Wilhelm Friedrich Hegel, *Lectures on the Philosophy of World History, Introduction: Reason in History*, trans. H.B. Nisbet (Cambridge: Cambridge University Press, 1975). For Hegel's revision of Christianity, see 36–65. See also *Hegel's Philosophy of Nature: Being Part Two of the Encyclopaedia of the Philosophical Sciences (1830)*, trans. A.V. Miller (Oxford: Clarendon Press, 1970).

63   George W. Bush, "2005 State of the Union Address," www.cnn.com/2005/ALLPOLITICS/02/02/sotu.transcript/.

64   Karl Marx and Friedrich Engels, *The Communist Manifesto*, trans. Paul M. Sweezy (New York: Monthly Review Press, 1964), 13.

65   This point was recently made once again—approvingly—by Paul Le Blanc in *Marx, Lenin, and the Revolutionary Experience: Studies of Communism and Radicalism in the Age of Globalization* (New York: Routledge, 2006). Not only does Le Blanc acknowledge that some of Marxism's "deepest roots" lie in the "Judeo-Christian tradition," but he calls for a renewed synthesis, a Christian Leninism (221–58, at 222). See also Giorgio Agamben, *The Time that Remains: A Commentary on the Letter to the Romans*, trans. Patricia Dailey (Stanford: Stanford University Press, 2005); Alain Badiou, *Saint Paul: The Foundation of Universalism*, trans. Ray Brassier (Stanford: Stanford University Press, 2003); and Slavoj Žižek, *The Puppet and the Dwarf: The Perverse Core of Christianity* (Cambridge: MIT Press, 2003).

66   Nicolas Berdyaev, *The Origin of Russian Communism* (Ann Arbor: University of Michigan Press,1960), 10.

67   David Redles, *Hitler's Millennial Reich: Apocalyptic Belief and the Search for Salvation* (New York: New York University Press, 2005), 188, and "Hitler as Messiah," 108–34.

68   Matthew 26:52; Luke 6:37; John 8:7; Matthew 5:39; Luke 6:31 (KJV).

69   See Robert W. Rydell, "Selling the World of Tomorrow: New York's 1939 World's Fair," *Journal of American History* 77:3 (December 1990): 966–70, and "The Iconography of Hope: The 1939–40 New York World's Fair," *American Studies at the University of Virginia*, xroads. virginia.edu/~1930s/DISPLAY/39wf/front.htm.

70   Joseph Schumpeter, *Capitalism, Socialism, and Democracy* (New York: Harper and Row, 1950), 81–86.

71   Rachel Carson, *Silent Spring* (Boston: Houghton Mifflin, 1962), 103–52.

72   See Linda J. Lear, *Rachel Carson: Witness for Nature* (New York: Henry Holt, 1997).

73   Lynn White, Jr., "The Historical Roots of Our Ecologic Crisis," *Science* 155 (March 10, 1967): 1203–7. An online version is available at www. uvm.edu/~gflomenh/ENV-NGO-PA395/articles/Lynn-White.pdf.

74　　International Standard Version.

75　　All passages from NIV.

76　　This passage is a summary of Strelan's observations by Michael McDow-
ell, "The Millennium Bug in Melanesia," *Journal of Asian Mission* 1:2
(September 1, 1999): 141–59, at 143.

CHAPTER 3

77　　Actually this is an oversimplification for the purposes of comprehensi-
bility. According to Akira Sadakata, "during each great *kalpa*, the universe is destroyed by fire caused by...seven suns. Every eighth great kalpa
a more fearful flood destroys the universe and destroys all abodes up to
and including the Second Dhyāna heavens. When the universe has been
destroyed seven times by water, it is brought to an end the next time by
wind, which causes the destruction of all abodes up to and including the
Third Dhyāna heavens" (105). Akira Sadakata, *Buddhist Cosmology: Philosophy and Origins*, trans. Gaynor Sekimori (Tokyo: Kōsei Publishing
Company, 1997), 99–110. See also "The Realm of the Dhyāna Practi-
tioner" in Sadakata, 63–67, and Sheng Yen, *Orthodox Chinese Buddhism*
(Berkeley: North Atlantic Books, 2007), 103–6. Needless to say, this
whole system contravenes what the Buddha taught in the Pali sutras (see
note 78 below).

78　　See for example the *Cūlamālunkya Sutta* 8:

> Therefore... remember what I have left undeclared.... And
> what have I left undeclared? "The world is eternal"—I have
> left undeclared. "The world is not eternal"—I have left unde-
> clared. "The world is finite"—I have left undeclared. "The
> world is infinite"—I have left undeclared....
>
> Why have I left that undeclared? Because it is unbenefi-
> cial, it does not belong to the fundamentals of the holy life, it
> does not lead to disenchantment, to dispassion, to cessation, to
> peace, to direct knowledge, to enlightenment, to Nibbāna.
> This is why I have left it undeclared.

The Middle Length Discourses of the Buddha: A New Translation of the Majjhima Nikāya, trans. Bhikkhu Ñānamoli and Bhikkhu Bodhi (Boston: Wisdom Publications, 1995), 533–36, at 536.

79   This prediction comes from the *Vinaya Pitaka.* See Tenth Khandhaka, Chapter 1, "On the Duties of Bhikkhunîs," in T.W. Rhys Davids and Herman Oldenberg, *Vinyaya Texts*, Part III, Kullavagga, IV–XII, www.sacred-texts.com/bud/sbe20/sbe20092.htm.

80   Mu Soeng, *The Diamond Sutra: Transforming the Way We Perceive the World* (Boston: Wisdom Publications, 2000), Section 6, 92.

81   *The Lotus Sutra: A Contemporary Translation of a Buddhist Classic*, trans. Gene Reeves (Boston: Wisdom Publications, 2008), 257.

82   Engo Kokugon, Case 29, "Daizui's It Will Be Gone With the Other," *Hekiganroku*, in *Two Zen Classics: Mumonkan and Hekiganroku*, trans. Katsuki Sekida (New York: Weatherhill, 1977), 223.

83   Albert E. Brumley, "I'll Fly Away," www.bluegrasslyrics.com/gospel_song.cfm-recordID=s07622.htm. Brumley's inspiration was 1 Thessalonians 4:16–17.

84   The often quoted phrase is from Exodus 2:22.

85   Luke 9:57–65 (NIV).

86   Ariyapariyesanā Sutta 18, in *The Middle Length Discourses*, 260.

87   *Dhammapada* 11:153–54. Gil Fronsdal, trans, *The Dhammapada: A New Translation of a Buddhist Classic with Annotations* (Boston: Shambhala, 2005), 40–41. See also the translation by Thanissaro Bhikkhu at tipitaka.wikia.com/wiki/Jaravagga.

88   Rick Warren, *The Purpose Driven Life: What on Earth Am I Here For* (Grand Rapids, MI: Zondervan, 2002). So far the book has sold more than twenty-six million copies.

89   See Matthew 17:20: "And Jesus said unto them, Because of your unbelief: for verily I say unto you, If ye have faith as a grain of mustard seed, ye shall say unto this mountain, Remove hence to yonder place; and it shall remove; and nothing shall be impossible unto you" (KJV).

90   Mahā-Assapura Sutta 21, in *The Middle Length Discourses*, 370.

91   Engo Kokugon, Case 8, "Suigan's Eyebrows," *Hekiganroku*, in *Two Zen Classics*, 169.

92   Mu Soeng, 135.

93   See *Matthew* 6:19–20: "Do not store up for yourselves treasures on earth, where moth and rust destroy and where thieves break in and steal. But store up for yourselves treasures in heaven" (NIV).

94   Friedrich Nietzsche, *The Antichrist,* Book 1, section 22, in Walter Kaufmann, trans., *The Portable Nietzsche* (New York: Penguin Books, 1959), 590.

95   Burton Watson, trans., *The Zen Teachings of Master Lin-chi: A Translation of the Lin-chi Lu* (Boston: Shambhala Publications, 1993), 25–26.

96   The status of non-being was much contested in Greek thought. The Greek word χάος, Kaos, actually meant nothingness, and Hesiod describes the world as emerging from it. Pythagoras and Heraclitus both apparently accepted its existence, while Parmenides did not. Plato's *Sophist* is really an argument against Parmenides and in favor of the necessity of non-being. Nevertheless, non-being remained merely a category of analysis for Greek civilization. In Genesis, God creates the world *ex nihilo*, from nothing, but after Creation nothingness is no longer present in the world.

97   See Lee Smolin, *The Life of the Cosmos* (New York: Oxford University Press, 1997), esp. 75–106. See also Joel Smoller and Blake Temple, "Shock-wave Cosmology inside a Black Hole," *Proceedings of the National Academy of Sciences*, 100.20 (September 30, 2003): 11216–11218, www.pnas.org/cgi/content/abstract/100/20/11216.

98   See Stephen Hawking, *A Brief History of Time* (New York: Bantam, 1998): "the total energy of the universe is exactly zero" (129).

99   *Ariyapariyesanā Sutta*, 6–11, in *In the Buddha's Words: An Anthology of Discourses from the Pāli Canon*, ed. Bhikkhu Bodhi (Boston: Wisdom Publications, 2005), 55

100   *Ariyapariyesanā Sutta*, 19–20 in *The Middle Length Discourses*, 260–61. Translation altered.

CHAPTER 4

101   Jake Warga, Commentary: "Saving the World in Ethiopia One Child at a Time," National Public Radio, 30 January 2007, www.npr.org/

templates/player/mediaPlayer.html?action=1&t=1&islist=false&id=
7085617&m=7085619.

102   G.W.F. Hegel, *The Philosophy of History*, trans. J. Jibree (New York:
       Dover, 1956), 99.

103   Mumon Ekai, Case 48, "Kempō's One Road," *Mumonkan, The Gateless
       Gate*, www.sacred-texts.com/bud/zen/mumonkan.htm.

104   *The Perfection of Wisdom in 700 Lines* in *Perfection of Wisdom: The Short
       Prajñāpāramita Texts*, trans. Edward Conze (Totnes, UK: Buddhist Pub-
       lishing Group, 2002), 126–27.

105   *The Perfection of Wisdom*, 129: "If in the four corners of the great ocean
       four men were to take water out of it, all that water which they take out
       would have one and the same taste, i.e., a salty taste; just so, Mañjuśrī,
       whatever demonstration of dharma has been demonstrated by me, all that
       has one single taste only, i.e., the taste of nonproduction, of nonexistence,
       of dispassion, of emancipation."

106   1 Timothy 6:12 (KJV).

107   In the United States the best example is the twelfth century statue in the
       Nelson-Atkins Museum of Art, in Kansas City, Missouri.

108   See *The Lankāvatāra Sūtra: A Māhayāna Text*, trans. Daisetz Teitaro
       Suzuki (New Delhi: Munshiram Manoharlal Publishers, 2003). There
       the Buddha says, "words are subject to birth and destruction; they are
       unsteady, mutually conditioning, and are produced by the law of causa-
       tion" (77).

109   *Lankāvatāra Sūtra*, 271.

110   See Suzuki, "Introduction," *Lankāvatāra Sūtra*, xxiii–xxx, also 17–21. In
       the Sutra, the unconscious Buddha mind, the Ālaya, is compared to an
       ocean and its Vijñānas, which produce discrimination, to its waves (42).
       This understanding of the mind has been a key element of Zen for more
       than a thousand years and of the Mahayana for even longer. See, for exam-
       ple, *The Awakening of Faith: Attributed to Aśvaghosha*, trans. Yoshito S.
       Hakeda (New York: Columbia University Press, 2006), 51–55, and Hsu
       Yun's teisho on the fourth day of a sesshin held in 1953 at the Jade
       Buddha monastery in Shanghai, in *Ch'an and Zen Teaching, First Series*,
       trans. Lu K'uan Yü (Berkeley, CA: Shambhala, 1970), 62–66.

111   For a biography of Gempo Roshi see Audrey Yoshiko Seo, *The Art of Twentieth-Century Zen: Paintings and Calligraphy by Japanese Masters* (Boston: Shambhala, 1998), 93–107.

112   This saying originally comes from the Chinese master Dahong Zuzheng. See Andrew Ferguson, *Zen's Chinese Heritage: The Masters and Their Teaching* (Boston: Wisdom Publications, 2000), 453.

113   "What a Wonderful World," George David Weiss and Bob Thiele. For Armstrong's performance on YouTube see www.youtube.com/watch?v=vnRqYMTpXHc.

114   "Soju's Verses on Oryu's Three Barriers," *Mumonkan*, in *Two Zen Classics*, 139–40.

115   *Lao Tzu's Taoteching*, trans. Red Pine (San Francisco: Mercury House, 1996), chapter 8, 16.

116   Mumon Ekai, Case 14, "Nansen Cuts the Cat in Two," *Mumonkan*, in *Two Zen Classics*, 58–61, at 58.

CHAPTER 5

117   *Divine Stories: Divyāvadāna*, trans. Andy Rotman (Boston: Wisdom Publications, 2008), 76, 192.

118   "The Internationale," Modern History Sourcebook, July 5, 2008, www.fordham.edu/halsall/mod/internat.html

119   Mumon Ekai, Case 35, "Seijo's Soul Separated," in *Two Zen Classics*, 106–8.

120   Genesis 3.

121   Romans 7:21–24 (NIV).

122   1 Corinthians 13:12 (NIV).

123   *Two Zen Classics*, 106.

124   Romans 7:24 (NIV).

125   *The Essential Chuang Tzu*, trans. Sam Hamill and J.P. Seaton (Boston: Shambhala, 1999), 1.

126   Ibid., 2.

127   "To admire antiquity and despise the present—this is the fashion of scholars.... Only the Perfect Man can wander the world without taking sides....

The great forests, the hills and mountains excel man in the fact that their growth is irrepressible." *The Essential Zhuanhzi: Basic Writings*, trans. Burton Watson (New York: Columbia University Press, 2003), 139–40.

128   Eihei Dōgen, "The Time-Being: Uji," in *Moon in a Dewdrop: Writings of Zen Master Dōgen*, ed. Kazuki Tanahashi (San Francisco: North Point Press, 1985), 76–83. See also www.thezensite.com/ZenTeachings/Dogen_Teachings/Uji_Welch.htm.

129   As Dōgen writes, "The time-being of all beings throughout the world in water and on land is just the actualization of your complete effort right now. All beings of all kinds in the visible and invisible realms are the time-being actualized by your complete effort, flowing due to your complete effort. Closely examine this flowing; without your complete effort right now, nothing would be actualized, nothing would flow." *Moon in a Dewdrop*, Section 13, 80.

130   John 18:36.

131   Walter Benjamin, "On the Concept of History," in *Walter Benjamin, Selected Writings, Vol. 4: 1938–1940*, trans. Harry Zohn (Cambridge: Harvard University Pres, 2003), 392–93. See also walterbenjamin.ominiverdi.org/wp-content/walterbenjamin_concepthistory.pdf.

132   "The Parable of the Plants," *The Lotus Sutra*, 159–68, at 162–63.

133   Baizhang, *The Treatise of the Samadhi of the Precious King*, in Nan Huai-Chin, *Basic Buddhism: Exploring Buddhism and Zen* (York Beach, ME: Samuel Weiser, 1997), 216–18, at 217.

CHAPTER 6

134   Engo Kokugon, Case 21, "Chimon's Lotus Flower and Lotus Leaves," *Hekiganroku*, in *Two Zen Classics*, 202–3, at 203.

135   Paul Krugman, "How Did Economists Get It So Wrong?" *New York Times*, 6 September 2009, www.nytimes.com/2009/09/06/magazine/06Economic-t.html.

136   See Paul Fussell, *The Great War and Modern Memory* (New York: Oxford University Press, 1977). As Fussell observes, "the Great War [WWI] was more ironic than any before or since. It was a hideous embarrassment to

the prevailing Meliorist myth which had dominated the public consciousness for a century. It reversed the idea of Progress" (8).

137   Han-shan Te-ching, "Essentials of Practice and Enlightenment for Beginners," trans. Guo-gu Shi, www.angelfire.com/electronic/awakening101/essentials.html.

138   What Dan Lusthaus says of the Yogācāra tradition holds true for Zen as well: "Tellingly, no Indian Yogācāra text ever claims that the world is created by mind. What they do claim is that we mistake our projected interpretations of the world for the world itself." *Buddhist Phenomenology: A Philosophical Investigation of Yogācāra Buddhism and the Ch'eng Wei-shih lun* (London: RoutledgeCurzon, 202), 534.

139   In his commentary on the *Sutra of Complete Enlightenment*, Te-Ch'ing quotes these lines from the Surangama Sutra:

> In utter serenity the bright light penetrates and reaches
> Everywhere (while) shining stillness encloses the great void:
> Then contemplating worldly things they all appear
> As nothing but illusions seen in dreams.

Ch-an and Zen Teaching, Third Series, ed. and trans. Lu K'uan Yü (Berkeley, CA: Shambhala, 1962), 269.

140   *The Poetry of Enlightenment*, trans. and ed. Sheng Yen (Elmhurst, NY: Dharma Drum Publications, 1987), 88. This poem comes from Te-Ch'ing's autobiography. Sheng Yen translates the first line as "the ten thousand manifestations" but the more conventional translation would be "ten thousand things."

141   See Red Pine's introduction to the poems of Te-Ch'ing in *The Clouds Should Know Me By Name: Buddhist Poet Monks of China*, ed. Red Pine and Mike O'Connor (Boston: Wisdom Publications, 1998), 114–16. See also Sung-peng Hsu, *A Buddhist Leader in Ming China: The Life and Thought of Han-shan Te-ch'ing* (University Park: Pennsylvania State University Press, 1979).

142   Chien-Chih Seng-T'san, "Hsin Hsin Ming" ("Faith in Mind"), trans. Richard B. Clarke, in *Faith Mind Inscription*, www.sacred-texts.com/bud/zen/fm/fm.htm.

143   T.S. Eliot, "The Hollow Men," http://aduni.org/~heather/occs/
       honors/Poem.htm.

CHAPTER 7

144   Jack Kerouac, *On the Road* (New York: Penguin Books, 2003), 181.

145   "Translator's Preface," *The Collected Songs of Cold Mountain*, trans. Red
       Pine (Port Townsend, WA: Copper Canyon Press, 2000), 3–18, at 3.

146   *The Poems of Cold Mountain*, 26, in *The Collected Songs of Cold Moun-
       tain*, 53.

147   "Hsin Hsin Ming," trans. Richard B. Clarke, in *Faith Mind Inscription*.

148   Matsuo Basho, *The Narrow Road to the Deep North and Other Travel
       Sketches*, trans. Nobuyuki Yuasa (Baltimore: Penguin Books, 1966), 97.

149   R.H. Blyth translation, www.haikupoetshut.com/basho1.html.

150   Mumon Ekai, Case 2, "Hyakyujo's Fox," *Mumonkan*, www.sacred-texts.
       com/bud/zen/mumonkan.htm.

151   Shunryu Suzuki, *Zen Mind, Beginner's Mind: Informal Talks on Medita-
       tion and Practice* (New York: Weatherhill, 1970), 130.

152   *The Zen Teachings of Master Lin-chi: A Translation of the Lin-chi Lu*,
       trans. Burton Watson (New York: Columbia University Press, 1999),
       52.

153   *The Zen Teachings of Lin-chi*, 85.

154   *The Vimalakirti Sutra*, trans. Burton Watson (New York: Columbia
       University Press, 1997), 78. This reference come from chapter six,
       which begins when the multitude of followers arrive and Shariputra
       observes that there are no chairs in Vimalakirti's little room. Then
       Vimalakirti answers, "a seeker of the Law [dharma] doesn't concern
       himself even about life or limb, much less about a seat! A seeker of the
       Law seeks nothing in the way of form, perception, conception, volition,
       or consciousness; he seeks nothing in the way of sense-realms or sense-
       media; he seeks nothing in threefold world of desire, form, and form-
       lessness" (75).

155   Genesis 3:7–11 (KJV).

CONCLUSION

156　　Dōgen says, "Firewood becomes ash, and it does not become firewood again. Yet, do not suppose that the ash is future and the firewood past. You should understand that firewood abides in the phenomenal expression of firewood, which fully includes past and future and is independent of past and future. Ash abides in the phenomenal expression of ash, which fully includes future and past." In the same way, "birth is an expression complete this moment. Death is an expression complete this moment. They are like winter and spring. You do not call winter the beginning of spring, nor summer the end of spring." Tanahashi, 70–71.

157　　*The Maha Prajna Paramita Hrdaya Sutra*, Kwan Um Zen School of Zen, www.kwanumzen.org/practice/chants/heartsutraenglish.html.

158　　Prajna Paramita, the wisdom that arises from emptiness "is able to relieve all suffering and [this] is true, not false."

159　　All beings are primarily Buddhas.
　　　　It is like water and ice:
　　　　There is no ice apart from water;
　　　　There are no Buddhas apart from beings.

　　　　Hakuin's Song of Zazen, trans. D.T. Suzuki, www.poetry-chaikhana. com/H/Hakuin/HakuinsSongo.htm.

160　　Engo Kokugon, Case 41, "Joshu and the Great Death," in *Two Zen Classics*, 258–59.

161　　"The Law of Kamma," in *In the Buddha's Words: An Anthology of Discourses from the Pāli Canon*, ed. Bhikkhu Bodhi (Boston: Wisdom Publications, 2005), 155–66, at 155.

162　　See Garrett Hardin, "The Tragedy of the Commons," *Science* 162:3859 (2003): 1243–48.

163　　Xinggang, "Meditation Cushion," in Beata Grant, *Daughters of Emptiness: Poems of Chinese Buddhist Nuns* (Boston: Wisdom Publications, 2003), 74.

INDEX

ABOUT THE AUTHOR

 KURT SPELLMEYER is an award-winning teacher and scholar in the English department at Rutgers University. He was also authorized to teach Zen by Kangan Glenn Webb in 1985, and now leads the Cold Mountain Sangha in New Jersey. He is the author of *Arts of Living: Reinventing the Humanities for the Twenty-first Century* and *Common Ground: Dialogue, Understanding, and the Teaching of Composition*, and the co-author of *The New Humanities Reader*.

ROBERT A.F. THURMAN is the Jey Tsong Khapa Professor of Indo-Tibetan Buddhist Studies at Columbia University, and the president of Tibet House US. He is the author of *Why The Dalai Lama Matters*, the volume *Anger* in Oxford University Press' *Seven Deadly Sins* series, and many other books. He was chosen by *TIME* as one of the twenty-five most influential people.

ABOUT WISDOM

WISDOM PUBLICATIONS, a nonprofit publisher, is dedicated to making available authentic works relating to Buddhism for the benefit of all. We publish books by ancient and modern masters in all traditions of Buddhism, translations of important texts, and original scholarship. Additionally, we offer books that explore East-West themes unfolding as traditional Buddhism encounters our modern culture in all its aspects. Our titles are published with the appreciation of Buddhism as a living philosophy, and with the special commitment to preserve and transmit important works from Buddhism's many traditions.

To learn more about Wisdom, or to browse books online, visit our website at www.wisdompubs.org.

You may request a copy of our catalog online or by writing to this address:

Wisdom Publications
199 Elm Street
Somerville, Massachusetts 02144 USA
Telephone: 617-776-7416
Fax: 617-776-7841
Email: info@wisdompubs.org
www.wisdompubs.org